When Black Starts to Crack

Parental Caregiving in the Black Community

African American caregivers are typically the only unpaid caregiver helping the recipient and more provide care in isolation, meaning no unpaid or paid help.

Caregiving in the U.S. – Fact Sheet – The "Typical" African American Caregiver, National Alliance for Caregiving and AARP, 2020

When Black Starts to Crack

Parental Caregiving in the Black Community

Edited by Gloria H. Rease, MDiv

ISBN: 979-8-9858056-0-4

Contents

Contents

Preface

Many of us have heard the idioms "Black don't crack" or "Good black don't crack." Usually, the phrase refers to the fact that a person of African descent does not look their chronological age. It also refers to resilience—that in the face of tragedy or overcoming obstacles, the person emerged looking pretty good. The downside of this ideology is that we tend to overlook the "cracks" that are forming right in front of our eyes, especially as it relates to family members in general and parents in particular. Emotional and physical cracks are a natural part of life. They may appear due to mental health unwellness, natural formations due to aging, or the lack of personal self-care. And they can happen at any time. It is important to be cognizant of the cracks that form in our lives because recognition gives us permission to seek appropriate help, stop or decrease the damage to ourselves and our families, and help us to heal and grow stronger. As suggested by this book's title, not all cracks are negative. Sometimes cracks bring forth new things: a stronger relationship between mother and daughter; bonding between a father and son; exposure of superficial cracks that, with a little bit of care, can be repaired.

This book is a collection of stories that address the experience of parental caregiving in the Black community. It explores ways in which caring for a parent, regardless of age, has many celebratory moments and

enormous challenges. These stories are a brief look at caregiving through the lens of parental care in the context of a Black experience. Contained herein are 13 uniquely beautiful stories (including my own) and six heartfelt artistic expressions about the experience of caregiving for a parent.

Within the last 25 years, research about informal caregiving[1] has grown exponentially. A great deal of attention is being placed on caregiving as the U.S. population of "Baby Boomers" age and are deciding to age in place. Issues like caregiver resources, psychological distress, and financial burden are all gaining traction as topics of discussion in the policy making arena.

Stakeholders and advocacy groups have lobbied Congress for decades to enact policies that address issues specific to the booming population of American family caregivers, resulting in passage of the RAISE Family Caregivers Act of 2017 (P.L. 115-119)[2]. The Act established the RAISE Family Caregiving Advisory Council (Advisory Council) that determined it was necessary to develop a strategy to

---

[1] Informal caregiving is the unpaid care and support family members and friends voluntarily provide individuals who are unable to function independently. Cook SK, Snellings L, Cohen SA. "Socioeconomic and Demographic Factors Modify Observed Relationship Between Caregiving Intensity and Three Dimensions of Quality of Life in Informal Adult Children Caregivers". Health Qual Life Outcomes. 2018 Aug 29;16(1):169. doi: 10.1186/s12955-018-0996-6. PMID: 30157852; PMCID: PMC6116379.

[2] *2022 National Strategy to Support Family Caregivers*, RAISE Act Family Caregivers Advisory Council and the Advisory Council to Support Grandparents Raising Grandchildren, 2022

address the complex issues of family caregivers. In September 2021, the Advisory Council released its initial report to Congress that proposed several recommendations for communities as well as federal, state, and local governments. One year later, on September 21, 2022, a joint report by the RAISE Act Family Advisory Council and the Advisory Council to Support Grandparents Raising Grandchildren released the *2022 National Strategy to Support Family Caregivers* with the purpose of ensuring resources were available to help family caregivers "maintain their own health, well-being, and financial security while providing crucial support to others."[3]

In their 2020 report, *Caregiving in the U.S.*, the National Alliance for Caregiving and AARP state that at least 53 million Americans were providing informal care to a family member in 2019. In that report, they surveyed or interviewed a total of 1,392 respondents: 61% White; 17% Hispanic/Latino; 14% African American; 5% Asian and 5% who identified as "Other." Of those caregiving respondents, 39% were men and 61% women. The male/female caregiver breakdown for African Americans was 34% men and 66% women with most of those caregivers caring for a parent or a parent-in-law. Clearly, women are carrying the burden of caregiving in all communities; however, it is especially true in the Black community. According to one study, "the historical need for informal support as a means of individual and group survival and...

---

[3] Ibid

intergenerational helping roles"[4] attributes to the phenomenon of Black women caring for parents in disproportionate numbers. Others have ascribed the disparity of Black women caregiving as a societal norm: caregiving is Black women's work.

In their 2020 report, the National Alliance of Caregivers and AARP found that the majority of Black caregivers tend to be women. Other research found that the primary motivation for providing care mainly stems from a sense of obligation to the parent.[5] Although this may be the fuel for some caregivers who submitted their journeys for this book, no one specifically stated that obligation was their motivating factor. What is most prevalent in the stories is that no formal plan was in place that addressed who would be responsible for parental care when the need arose, regardless of whether the need was due to aging, mental illness, or physical disability. For the most part, these authors just stepped in to provide whatever care was needed.

When interviewing Black caregivers, researchers found that respondents felt they had no choice in taking on the caregiver role. This number is steadily on the incline. In 2009 the National Alliance for Caregiving and AARP reported that 43% of their interviewees indicated

---

[4] Thornton, N., & Hopp, F. P.. ""So I Just Took Over": African American Daughters Caregiving for Parents with Heart Failure". Families in Society, 92(2), 211–217. https://doi.org/10.1606/1044-3894.4103, 2011

[5] Le, Ocean and Boddie, Angie. "It's Time to Meet the Needs of African American and Black Caregivers" American Society on Aging, Generations Today, Nov-Dec 2020

they had no choice[6] and that number increased to 50% in their 2020 report. The 2020 report and other research also indicated that most Black caregivers found meaning and purpose in their role as caregiver.[7] This fact is evident in some of the stories contained herein.

General distrust in the health care system and nursing homes specifically is the motivation for many Blacks to ensure their parents age in their homes. The COVID pandemic exposed the stark health disparities in communities of color.[8] The Centers for Disease Control and Prevention (CDC) reported that 23% of COVID related deaths in the United States were among long-term care facility patients and staff.[9] Couple that fact with historical maltreatment of Blacks in the cases of the U.S. Public Health Service syphilis experiment at Tuskegee and the secretive utilization of Henrietta Lacks' cells to develop new cancer treating technologies by John Hopkins Hospital, and you get generational leeriness towards medical institutions. This stance is evident in past and

---

[6] Caregiving in the U.S. - A Focused Look at the Ethnicity of Those Caring for Someone Age 50 or Older - Executive Summary, 2009

[7] Community and Culture Help Black Caregivers Cope with the Challenges of Family Caregiving. AARP, 2021

[8] For more information visit https://www.kff.org/report-section/racial-disparities-in-covid-19-key-findings-from-available-data-and-analysis-issue-brief/

[9] https://www.cdc.gov/nhsn/covid19/ltc-report-overview.html

current research and interviews with Black caregivers,[10],[11] and contributes to the high number of family caregivers in the Black community.

Many of the caregivers who participated in surveys and interviews looked to their faith for strength to persevere during their challenges with caregiving.[12] One of the contributing authors to this publication viewed her journey as part of God's plan for her and her mother. Faith is the thread that weaves throughout many of the stories and artistic expressions presented here. It appears to make the burden lighter for some and raises questions for others.

It is hoped that through this book readers can celebrate the cracks of life, adapt to their existence, become better caregivers to their parents, and learn to exercise some self-care during their journeys.

---

[10] Lampley-Dallas VT, Mold JW, Flori DE. "Perceived needs of African-American caregivers of elders with dementia". J Natl Med Assoc. 2001 Feb;93(2):47-57. PMID: 12653382; PMCID: PMC2640631.

[11] Le, Ocean and Boddie, Angie.

[12] Janevic, Mary R., and Connell, Cathleen M. Connell, "Racial, Ethnic, and Cultural Differences in the Dementia Caregiving Experience": Recent Findings, 2001.

About the Editor

Gloria H. Rease is a retired entrepreneur, U.S. Army veteran, mother of one, and grandmother of two. She has a Bachelor of Arts degree in Business from Trinity College (Washington, DC) and Master of Divinity degree from Fuller Theological Seminary (Pasadena, CA). For pleasure, she enjoys reading, basketball, tennis, jigsaw puzzles, Alvin Ailey Dance Company performances, watching "The Hair Tales" and "Queen Sugar," theater, visits to most art galleries, graphic design, and promoting Black history and culture.

Since 2011, she has resided in Alexandria, VA with her 95-year-old mother, who she has the pleasure of watching age ever so gracefully in the home while Gloria provides care as her adult child caregiver.

I RELEASE AND I LET GO

Rickie Byars and Michael Beckwith
(permission granted)

SOLO

There was a time in my life I thought I had to do it all for myself
And I didn't know the grace of God was sufficient
And I didn't know the love of God was at hand

But now I can say
If you are discouraged
Struggling just to make it through another day
You got to let it go, let it all go
And this is what you have to say

CHORUS

I release and I let go
I let the Spirit run my life
And my heart is open wide
Yes, I'm only here for God

No more struggle, no more strife
With my faith I see the light
I am free in the Spirit
Yes, I'm only here for God

Contributors

Alice A. Brown

Alice is an entrepreneur and consultant and is the owner of Brown Business Services, LLC. She credits her mother with helping to shape her career as diversity manager, housing workforce developer, and elder care aide by demonstrating love for humankind, showing empathy, being nonjudgmental, and advocating for others. Alice is the 5th of 8 children; she is a resident of Alexandria, Virginia.

Hank and Charlene Davis

Hank and Charlene are currently living in Vienna, Austria. Charlene retired from the Department of Homeland Security and Hank is employed as a Technical Officer with the United Nations.

Kim El

Kim is a Pittsburgh-born playwright and educator. She earned her Bachelor of Arts degree in Journalism from Duquesne University. Kim has written 19 plays and is best known for the production of her one-woman show, Straightening Combs." She currently lives in Braddock, Pennsylvania.

Marcia V. Ellis

Marcia is the Community Coordinator for the DC Center for AIDS Research at the George Washington University. Marcia and her mother live in Alexandria, Virginia.

Shimoda Donna Emanuel

Shimoda is the principal creative for Shimoda Accessories. She is a mixed-media artist who creates jewelry and fiber art for the soul. Shimoda recently self-published her second book, <u>Sacred Stitches: The Art of Caregiving. Tips for Stitching Yourself Together When Caring for Someone with Alzheimer's</u>. Her jewelry and art are available for

purchase at the gift shop of The Smithsonian National Museum of African American History and Culture.

Reverend Brenda Grier-Miller

Rev. Grier-Miller is Associate Dean of Students Emerita, Oberlin College. She is ordained with the House of the Lord Churches, Prelate Leah Daughtry. Rev. Grier-Miller serves in ministry with her husband of 45 years, A.G. Miller, Pastor at The Oberlin House of the Lord Fellowship. She was raised in Brooklyn, New York and is a product of the New York City public school system. Rev. Grier-Miller is educated and trained as a Social Worker, BSW and MSSA (Adelphi University and CSWU). She and her husband are blessed with four adult children, with three wonderful spouses and four grandchildren. They live in Oberlin, Ohio.

Dorothy J. James

Dorothy is a Spiritual Director living in Marina del Rey, California. She is a business owner who runs a corporate and tax agency specializing in the nonprofit world of spiritual and healing music and performing arts. Dorothy is a Spiritual Director and Practitioner of spiritual healing through the African Diaspora of traditional spirituality and healing.

Monique S. Johnson, PhD

Monique is an executive leader with a mission-driven enterprise. She is passionate about solving complex problems, making operational improvements, building high-performance teams, and mentoring next generation leaders in her professional and personal worlds. Monique and her family live in Richmond, Virginia.

Ivy A. Lewis

Ivy lives in Upper Marlboro, Maryland and is a community planner who currently serves as a director of a small public works agency. In addition, Ivy is an entrepreneur and gifted designer of unique jewelry.

Dyone Massey Mitchell
Dyone is a Legal Assistant with the United States Department of Justice. She enjoys hand dancing with her husband of 31 years, Charles Mitchell. Dyone is an active member of the Freestyle Dances; Vice President of the nonprofit group Giving Others A Dream, and a member of Delta Sigma Theta Sorority. She and her husband live in Suitland, Maryland.

E. Bonita Mitchell
Bunni is a retired federal government employee, residing in Washington, DC. She is a graduate of LaCase School of Business and attended Federal City College, Howard University, Agriculture Graduate School, and University of the District of Columbia.

Lesa Moore
Lesa lives in Oxon Hill, MD and is employed as a Legal Administrative Assistant. Her passions include diversity, equity, and inclusion.

Pamela Ferrell Neal
Pamela is a hair and health subject matter expert. Over the past 30+ years she is responsible for changing state laws to protect African American women's rights to open natural haircare businesses and wear their natural hair in the workplace. Pamela lives in Washington, D.C.

Rayetta Wheeler-Rice
Rayetta is a retired Maywood Public Library employee. Rayetta is the eldest of six children. In addition to her three children, she is also "mother" to one nephew and grandmother of four. An avid vegetable and flower gardener, she finds the activity to be cathartic and relaxing. Her mission in life is to help Seniors and youth in whatever way she can. Rayetta is a member of Rock of Ages Baptist Church in her hometown of Maywood, Illinois.

Kumea Shorter-Gooden, PhD
Kumea is a daughter, sister, wife, mother, grandmother, and auntie. She is the co-author of Shifting: The Double Lives of Black Women in America. Kumea is the principal owner of Shorter-Gooden Consulting, a consulting

firm that specializes in diversity, equity and inclusion consulting, coaching and training. She lives in Washington, DC with her husband.

Belinda Robinson Stanford

Belinda is a retired elementary school teacher/educator, who lives in Tinley Park, IL. Belinda states that she is a Believer in God and knows that His Son, Jesus died for her sins. As a Believer, she knows that with God's Love, Grace and Mercy she was gifted to be a caregiver for her mother.

Sound Whisdom

Sound Whisdom is also known as "Sound", "Mae", and "Whisdom" (Wholly-HIS-DOMain). She is a multifaceted independent artist/author/educator/ advocate. She is a founding member of the Fearless Storytellers Movement and the 40+ DDC Dallas SubClub. Sound is blessed to have the unwavering support of her husband and blended family of nine children. What makes her life most rewarding is knowing her life's mission: to model compassion and honor the purpose in her life and in the lives of others.

Introduction

In Black and all ethnic communities, family member caregiving is an important topic to discuss. Despite all the available research and data analyses, my reason for writing this book was a very personal one: I am an adult child caregiver who was clueless about the obligations, challenges, resources, and opportunities associated with caring for a parent. I chose to focus on parental care in the Black community primarily because parental caregiving comes with its unique set of nuances in our community. For one thing, no matter what age, the adult child caregiver will always be the child in the mind of the parent, whether you are 8 or 80 years old. Some of us come from families where "children are seen and not heard" so there may be some difficulty challenging a parent even when you know what is in their best interest. Then there is the issue of sibling dynamics. Are you the eldest? What is the family pecking order? Will they or will they not assist with caregiving? All these questions informed my decision to collect these stories and publish this book.

I selected the Black community because it is MY community. In my community, we tend not to institutionalize our parents. For the most part, we view aging parents as our elders and when they transition, they become our ancestors. Additionally, for many Black families the decision to allow our parents to age in place is based on finances. According to

Genworth Financial 2021 Cost of Care Survey the median national monthly cost for assisted living facilities is $4,500 and for nursing homes a semi-private room is $7,908 and a private room is $9,034[13] per month. Not many of us can afford that monthly expense and oftentimes our parents do not have enough assets to carry that financial burden. Add all of this to the fact that most of us are not convinced that our parent will receive the best and most appropriate care in a nursing home[14] and you get many Black parents aging in place and being cared for by an adult child or other family member.

My journey towards the role of "caregiver" began in 2011 as the project manager for a home renovation for my mother's home. The house was nearly in total disrepair; her husband had died the previous year and my daughter, who was living in Los Angeles at the time, had discovered the Homeowners Rehabilitation Loan Program (HRLP)[15] that administered loans to eligible families for home renovations in Alexandria, VA. My daughter completed the application, Mother was

---

[13]   Genworth   Financial,   https://www.genworth.com/aging-and-you/finances/cost-of-care.html.

[14] "While Black and Hispanic nursing home residents tend to have poorer health, they are also less likely to get hospice care at the very end of their lives, receive worse pain management and are more likely to undergo aggressive treatment and hospitalization." Good End-of-Life Care Out of Reach for Many Black Nursing Home Residents. U.S. News, March 8, 2022.

[15] The Home Rehabilitation Loan Program is administered through the City of Alexandria, Office of Housing. For more information visit https://www.alexandriava.gov/housing-services/homeowner-resources

approved and now the City needed a designated "project manager," preferably a family member. It seemed like my job description. It was probably perfect timing since I was starting to get the itch to move from California and find my next adventure. It was to be a 6- to 8-month project; just enough time for me to figure out where I was going to put down roots for the next leg of my life. So I packed up my bags and headed to Alexandria.

Some people are born caregivers; it is just part of their DNA. They were stamped with CAREGIVING even before conception. I was not. I am not a natural caregiver. I am better known for giving you the tools necessary for self-sufficiency and pointing you in the right direction to achieve a goal. I believe in self-reliance with all my heart and soul. Just ask my daughter. I considered myself a loving and supportive parent during her formative years and wanted her to not depend on others for her ideas, opinions, and care. At an early age one of her responsibilities was to reconcile our checkbook. Her punishments were typewritten contracts that were posted on the refrigerator, outlining the infraction, clearly spelling out the consequences, delineating the beginning and end dates of her restrictions. So entering the role of caregiver for my aging mother was quite a shock to my system.

Initially, I figured I would just take Mother along on the ride of my life and fit her in between entrepreneurship, intimate and personal relationships, client projects and visits to museums and art galleries. Well, that did not work out too well. I found myself stressed and angered

by the fact that I had to adjust my schedules—work and play—to take care of her needs.

The first five years were an easy ride. I leased an office that was a 6-minute walk from the house; I scheduled her doctor's appointments and planned my schedule around them. I did the grocery shopping; she did the cooking. She did her own laundry. I turned a blind eye to the small indications that something more was happening. Then I remember this day as if it were yesterday: Mother called me on my cell phone hysterically crying and clearly very upset: "I can't find him! I've lost the little boy! I fell asleep and when I woke up the little boy was gone! I looked under the bed, and I cannot find him!" I tried to calm her down, but she was inconsolable. I was in the office, a short walk away, but I needed to get to her immediately, so I hopped in my car for a 3-minute drive to the house. When I arrived, she was sitting on the sofa, crying about having lost this little boy. I had no idea who she was talking about. We lived alone. There were no babies in our household—no children, no little boys. How do I handle this? I tried reasoning: "Mother, there are no children in the house; nobody lives here but you and me. We are the only ones here." Her response was, "Then I must be really losing my mind!" I tried calming her down by saying that perhaps it was just a dream and sometimes our dreams appear so real that when we awake, we feel as though it was reality. She gave me that "you're-just-trying-to-play-me" look but kept quiet. I was able to finally, somehow, get her calmed down. However, I instinctively knew this was the beginning of a new phase for us. I had not yet incorporated the term "caregiver" into my vocabulary or

thought processes, but that is where I was headed and I could no longer ignore the fact that dementia was residing in our home.

As mentioned earlier, my reasons for embarking on the journey to write this book are manifold. First, I would have benefitted so greatly from hearing stories of others in the early stages of my caregiving journey. I believe I would have been less frustrated and more fully aware of the anger, issues, and sense of isolation I was experiencing. I would have been more forgiving of myself. Parental caregiving is a wonderful experience, but not without challenges. Some embark on it as part of a long-term plan of care, others of us just happen upon it.

I believe some anecdotal stories like the ones included here would have helped me to understand that I am not alone on this journey, that there are others who are experiencing similar situations. These stories would have shed some light on how others handled their challenges. I'm certain they would have made me more compassionate.

Had I known of a place to locate just a few of the myriad of resources I discovered along the way, I believe my experience would have been less arduous. I stumbled upon quite a few resources but many of them I had to dig for but not until I discovered the vocabulary required to search for them on the internet. It seems that the most needed resources are so well hidden that it takes a team of "caregiver archeologists" to unearth them. I am hopeful that the few mentioned herein will help someone along the way.

But even more than any of these, it is important to highlight and bring attention to the uniqueness of caring for parents in the Black

community. As much as we want to believe that parental caregiving is a universal experience, understanding that ethnic health care disparities exist—the research bears that out—helps us to understand the importance of advocating for appropriate health care for ourselves and others. Being able to discuss our distrust of the health care system, racial imbalances in care, and the economics of long-term and mental health care are sorely lacking in our community and is significant to the well-being of the Black community and our families.

I have basically supported my mother most of my adult life. Whether it was flying her in for a visit to whatever city I was living at the time for a long respite, ordering groceries to be delivered to her home when I lived 3,000 miles away and her cupboards were bare, making long distance calls to her doctors to discuss her plan of care, or paying her telephone bill each month for 15 years. I have been there for her emotionally, financially, and spiritually. Even so, at no point did we discuss any plan for caring for her as she aged. Perhaps, given the tumultuous life she lived with her alcoholic, abusive husband, it was enough for her to just make it to another day. Maybe she did not believe she was going to make it to an old age. And perhaps, I was too focused on loving her in the present that I gave little thought to caring for her in the future. At any rate, no plan was made. However, I believe that part of the reason is that many in our community, including myself, are so busy trying to survive in the here-and-now, that we rarely have the luxury of planning so far in advance. After all, we have bills to pay, racism to battle, and children to look after.

Caring for Mother has been an educational journey. I have learned so much about me, the health care system, Medicare and Medicaid, home health aides, and local resources available for seniors and persons with disabilities. I was certainly ill-prepared to deal with any of this. Hopefully this book will highlight some of these resources and will be a tool to equip other caregivers who are walking in, or about to walk in, the footsteps of these brave, blessed, and enlightened contributors.

Because the journey for me is a reflective one, I have included Reflective pages that will allow readers an opportunity to think about what they read, reflect on their journey, or think about plans for their eventual journey of being a caregiver recipient. I hope you will share your thoughts on these pages so you or your loved ones may be better prepared when the time arrives.

Music played a pivotal role in our lives throughout this caregiving experience. It was the tool I used to prepare Mother for a restful night; and it was my salvation in times of gratitude, anger, and stress. We didn't play a lot of music in the home. I just sang a bar or two from whatever song came to my mind at the time. Mind you, I am no songstress, and initially Mother would not join in because she said she couldn't sing. I assured her that anyone can make a joyful noise. Our singing seemed to calm us both and it became something Mother looked forward to at the end of her day. *I Release and I Let Go* (Rickie Byars and Michael Beckwith) is my daily mantra. It is the song that grounds me into the task of caregiving and gives me the strength to make it through the day. When it was difficult getting Mother up and going in the mornings, I may belt out

a few lines from James Brown's "Get Up"; she always smiled at the "shake your moneymaker" part. Mother's favorite bedtime song was "I Won't Complain" by Rev. Paul Jones. She also sang along with "Amazing Grace" and "You're the Best Thing That Ever Happened" (Gladys Knight). A lot of songs were instrumental in helping us get through some challenging and joy-filled moments.

In this book, the reader will find stories that I wish were available to me at the outset of my caregiving experience. Reading about or hearing stories of other caregivers would have been instrumental to my mental well-being. These stories or stories like them would have helped me recognize certain issues related to aging and memory care. I believe they would have helped me to understand that this path may be a lonely journey, but it is well worth the ride.

~ Gloria H. Rease, Editor

Caregiver Stories and Artistic Expressions

About the Back Cover

Because I am such a visual person, I wanted to provide a visual example of beauty in the mist of cracks. Which is a part of the essence of my poem. After searching and praying for the right visual, my friend, a local artisan Sheree Ferrato, posted the stained-glass panel that she had just completed. I thought the piece was exquisite and was a perfect visual of beauty out of broken pieces.

Serving as Pastor (my Husband) and Minister (myself) we have seen much death/dying and illness this year. It seems that many of our Elders, many whom have been the backbone of our homes, communities, and organizations, have laid down their "swords and shields" to study work no more. And those who serve as "Care Givers" have needed another level of support and hope during these times. This has been our experience both congregationally, communally, and in our personal family life.

I wanted my poem to serve as an encouragement, support, and comfort for those of us who have found ourselves in the positions of Care Givers.

As Care Givers, we have and are caring for precious jewels and gems and if taken the time, we can recognize and acknowledge those gems, through the "Cracks." ~ *Rev. Brenda Grier-Miller*

When Black Cracks

Brenda Grier-Miller

When black cracks
It transforms into a mosaic
Many pieces forming a new whole
With regular and irregular
Sized and shaped pieces
More than fragments
Sometimes entire chunks

Trying hard to hold it together
To show their ability,
competency, usefulness
To make sense of space, place,
and time
Old and new, past and present
Oh! Lord God, your mercies are
new every morning

It is the caregivers
The ones who are charged with
providing care—
Offsprings, spouses, relatives,
lovers, friends,
Neighbors, health care providers,
nurses, doctors,
Dietitians, therapists, spiritual
leaders and the like

They often hold the distinct
privilege
To serve as the mortar-spreaders,
Connecting and giving new space

As the cracks penetrate deeper
and expand
Holding the pieces together
Creating a beautiful continuum of
old and new

When black cracks
It creates the possibility
Of a broader platform
A space in which what was once
"whole"
Can be viewed from a clearer
vantage point

When black cracks
Do not be mistaken
To think that it's ending
It's only just begun to go on
This time when light shines
through it
The prisms spring forth
An even richer, brilliant, brighter
light

When black cracks
Watch carefully for
Priceless gems to emerge

Reflections

Driving Miss Daisy
Gloria H. Rease

My mother was born in 1927; she was the 13th and final child born to Edward Jr. and Annie Bruce in Pitt County, North Carolina. By the time she was born, one sister had died in a fire at the age of 2, and a few of her other siblings were adults, some with their own families. From what I gathered from family reunions and visits to the family home in North Carolina, Daisy was an independent, strong-willed individual; she spoke her mind and didn't care who did or did not like it. She forged her own path. When she was 24 years old, circa 1951, she designed and had constructed the family home in Williamston, NC on property her father purchased several years prior. She tells me she was motivated to have the home built to have a comfortable place for her parents to live and for her to raise her two young children with, I suspect, a third on the way. Although the home is no longer in the family, some 70 years later she still beats herself up for the way she designed it.

My memories of Carolina Avenue are peppered with the awe of witnessing how this huge family of 12 siblings got along so well. They laughed and cajoled each other; my uncles sang made up songs and told family stories; my aunts cooked and told them to stop lying. But the most astonishing part was watching how quickly my mother switched from being "citified" to "countrified." You see, mother and her new husband migrated from Williamston, NC to Alexandria, VA in 1958, taking her 5-

year-old baby (that's me) and leaving her three older children in the care of her parents and siblings while she got settled. Once settled, she would send for her other children. In Alexandria, she had no discernible accent but as soon as she got with her siblings all facades of city living fell away.

My aunt Nettie was my first example of a parental caregiver. After my grandmother became ill, Nettie moved into the family home to take care of both parents. Sometime after grandma died, Uncle Dick, who was a widower, and his four young children also moved into the home. I recall that Aunt Nettie ran that house like it was a well-oiled machine. Nobody messed with Aunt Nettie, and you would be advised not to come to her for advice if you were not prepared to hear the truth. She bathed "Poppa," as his children called him, in a big tin wash tub in the kitchen; she cleaned, cooked, laundered, and took no nonsense from anybody. Aunt Nettie was a prime example of how to manage a household and lovingly care for an aging parent. At the time I am certain that the word "caregiver" was nowhere in her mind. She provided care because that was her father and it is what was expected of her since she was the only unmarried, childless, female offspring. She never seemed disgruntled or remorseful about the responsibility; but then again, I only saw her in August when we drove "home" for family reunions. I was around 10 or 11 when my grandmother died and my grandfather died two and a half months before my 17th birthday.

A self-proclaimed "Miss Know It All," my mother started elementary school at the age of five and graduated high school alongside her sister Beulah who was two years older, the only two to get a high

school diploma. Determined not to clean the homes of white folks, Mother set her sight on moving to Alexandria, VA to join her eldest sister Phoebe and her uncle Jerry, her mother's brother. Before moving to Alexandria, mother received her cosmetology license from Sales Beauty College in Wilson, NC, where she drove 55 miles each day to attend classes. She often tells the story about lying about her age when she was sixteen to get a driver's license so she could run errands for her parents. According to legend, granddaddy owned an old Ford Model T with the crank in the front; there is no way now to verify that story since she is the last survivor of that family of 15.

Today, Mother is unable to get the details straight, so I'm not sure when she met her husband, Verlon Wise. Sometimes she says it was on the back porch of her home in Williamston, which is possible since Verlon's mother lived a few streets over. On another occasion she stated that they met while part of a cleaning crew at St. Agnes School for Girls in Alexandria. At any rate, they remained married until his death in 2010 after nearly 50+ years of his physical and verbal abuse, alcoholism, womanizing, and financial irresponsibility. Together they had one son, my baby brother.

Mother worked for a couple years as a domestic for an Alexandria white family. At some point she worked as part of the cleaning crew at Saint Agnes School for Girls. For a short while she worked in a beauty salon, however she always did hair on the side in the kitchen of her home. Her last official employment was with JC Penney as a Stock Clerk.

Around 1974 Mother was diagnosed with diabetes and shortly after, she left her JC Penney job. To bring income into the household, she began an in-home daycare. Most people will primarily remember her for providing care for their children while they went off to work. Even today, she is still in touch with some of the children and their parents and most consider her part of their families. They form the bulk of her community outside of the home. Many of them call to check on her and send birthday and holiday cards with updated pictures and announcements about her former child care recipients.

In 2011, while the home was being renovated and we were living in temporary housing, I shuttled mother to and from her many doctor appointments: endocrinologist, nephrologist, cardiologist, podiatrist, ophthalmologist, oncologist, primary care physician. I had to go toe-to-toe with a couple of her doctors just to treat her with human dignity. Her initial primary care physician hardly looked up from her computer during Mother's visits with her, and she was throwing out medical terminology that I did not understand and mother could not comprehend. After the second visit we changed physicians.

Mother's endocrinologist was the most helpful of all her doctors. While I was living in California, I practically talked to Mother daily or at least every other day. I would inquire about her health and ask about her blood sugar levels. She would tell me that it was "ok" and I would ask what the reading was and she generally responded that it was around 300 or so. Being ignorant to normal blood sugar levels, I did not think it was a problem since Mother told me it was "ok" and she had been

managing her diabetic care for the past couple of decades. After I relocated back to Virginia, my first visit to her endocrinologist was enlightening, to say the very least. She educated me about normal blood sugar levels, meal preparation, and how to manage Mother's diabetes. At our first meeting with Dr. Garcia, she adjusted her insulin dosage and gave instructions on how and when to check Mother's blood sugar levels. At the time, since Mother was in the office with me during the conversation with the doctor, I assumed that she would follow the instructions. But after a few weeks I realized she was not taking the proper dosage of insulin, she was eating all the wrong foods, and she was not checking her blood sugar levels as instructed. It dawned on me that she either did not hear or could not comprehend most of what Dr. Garcia had said. I quickly discovered that this was the case with all her doctors and contributed to the reason that her cardiologist was constantly increasing her medications. He assumed she was following his treatment plan and prescription dosages still her blood pressure was not being regulated, so he would just prescribe an additional medication. Meanwhile, the problem was that she was not taking his advice to minimize or eliminate salt from her diet, drink more water, or take daily walks.

My takeaway from those doctor visits was that there is a tremendous need for medical advocates for individuals who are unable to advocate for themselves, whether due to aging, cognitive impairment, hearing loss, or language barriers. It was important for me to sit in at doctor appointments to ensure that Mother was able to fully participate

in her treatment plans. Since she is always the worry wart, I also wanted her to understand that she, all factors considered, was in fairly good health.

One of the most important lessons I learned is that it's tough doing this alone. A healthy support system and knowledge about available resources is paramount. Local, state, and federal resources are hidden treasures, and I mean REALLY HIDDEN. It's as though they are intentionally buried so the people who need them most will never have access to them. If you do not have computer/internet access, or you do not know the right words to type in the Google search bar, you are just out of luck! There was no internet service in my Mother's home until 2011. She did not own a computer or a tablet and has never owned a cell phone. The household was technologically deficit. Strictly by happenchance, I discovered that my mother was eligible for the City of Alexandria Real Estate Tax Relief and Assistance Program for Elderly and Disabled Persons.[16] The eligibility age for the program is 65 years; when I became aware of the program mother was 84 years old and the property taxes, which were on a payment plan, were delinquent. Why on earth didn't anyone in the Real Estate Tax Office let them know that such a program existed? I will never know.

In 2018 I visited the City of Alexandria, Department of Community and Human Services, Division of Aging and Adult Services (DAAS) in

---

[16] To learn more about the program visit: https://www.alexandriava.gov/taxes/real-estate-tax-relief-and-assistance-program-for-elderly-and-disabled-persons

search of any resources that could assist Mother; they proved to be very helpful. She was eligible to receive free Glucerna deliveries due to the fact that she was starting to lose her appetite and was not eating properly. Additionally, they registered her for Meals on Wheels, however Mother refused to eat the food, so I asked them to stop the program. Also, through DAAS she qualified to receive home health aide services twice per week for two hours each day. This was a tremendous help since I was still working at the time and having someone to do her laundry and clean her bedroom and bathroom was a huge load off my shoulders. In 2019, her Family Services Specialist at DAAS felt that she may qualify for a Medicaid waiver due to progressive memory decline and made that recommendation to his supervisor. A team from DAAS came to the home to do an assessment and found that she met the qualifications that made her eligible for the Commonwealth Coordinated Care (CCC) Plus Waiver[17] based on need, due to cognitive impairment and other health conditions. This program allowed Mother to have a maximum of 56 hours per week of home health aide services, however after an in-person evaluation it was determined that she only required 49 hours. What a major benefit for us both!

Finding a reliable home health aide was the most difficult hurdle I had to overcome. Not all aides or home health agencies are the same. Before Mother became eligible for Medicaid we had a string of different

---

[17] To learn more about this State of Virginia program visit:
https://www.dmas.virginia.gov/for-members/managed-care-programs/ccc-plus/

home health aides providing services for the twice weekly services approved by DAAS. I was under the mistaken impression that aides assigned to us would know their job description, be reliable, conscientious and would arrive each day ready to work. Well, not so. I ran through many aides who simply thought their job was to babysit or provide companion care. But that was not the only thing on the list of tasks and duties provided by their agency (see Figure 1). The paperwork given to me by the agency representative included light housekeeping with a list of tasks per room. It was my expectation that in addition to monitoring my mother, the aide would perform those tasks. I was so frustrated about returning home and seeing tasks undone that I created a task list on my own (see Figure 2). I emailed it to the home care agency for approval, to ensure the tasks were accurate. Whenever I interviewed potential aides, we reviewed my Aides Task List, which was strictly based on what the health care agency outlined in their agreement. It was important to manage expectations; I wanted the aide to understand what was expected. Quite a few of them decided they were not willing to do more than sit and watch television.

The COVID-19 pandemic had a tremendous impact on us. Discussions about health disparities in the Black community and Mother's pre-existing chronic conditions caused me to be very cautious—I nearly wrapped her in cellophane! Two weeks before the pandemic shutdown I found an aide who appeared to be reasonably reliable. News of the pandemic began to surface without any clear guidelines about protocols; the shutdown happened and the aide was

unable to come for a few days. In the meanwhile, Mother was hospitalized for about five days. After her discharge I contacted the home health agency to ask for the aide to return but by this time she had found another client. Not sure about COVID and with no clear guidelines to follow, I decided to delay trying to find another aide until I had a better understanding of the appropriate Personal Protective Equipment (PPE) requirements and the potential health hazards. After nearly six months of being overwhelmed and stressed about providing 24-7 care for Mother, I was advised by her health insurance company representative that I could get paid through Medicaid for taking care of her. My choices were Consumer-Directed or Agency-Directed services.[18] So in July 2020, I chose Agency-Directed services, got certified as a home health aide, and became a paid employee of an agency. I selected this route because I felt certification would give me needed information and knowledge about how to properly care for Mother. But after about six months of being the only caregiver and being responsible for all meal preparation, laundry, cleaning, etc., I was completely and totally exhausted. Additionally, Mother's care needs were on the rise: she no longer cooked; she sometimes forgot how to inject her insulin; she wouldn't take her medications; and I could not leave her home alone for more than a couple of hours for fear she would do something dangerous or fall. Due to the pandemic, I had absolutely no social life; my creativity was completely

---

[18] With Consumer-Directed services the person using the services is allowed to select, hire, fire, and train their particular caregiver(s). An agency is responsible for hiring the caregiver with Agency-Directed services.

dried up; and I had shut down my business and was at home full-time. I was knee deep into caregiving and, as much as I loved my mother, I was desperately in need of an escape.

By January 2021, it appeared that concerns about COVID were lessening, and I felt more comfortable with the idea of letting someone into the home. I reached out to the home health agency I worked with and told them I was ready to be replaced by an aide. For months the agency told me they were looking but could not find an appropriate worker. In December 2021 I renovated our kitchen and was without full kitchen access for nearly 3 months, so I told the agency to put the health aide search on hold until after I finished that project. In March 2022 I told them to start looking again; the agency had the same excuses about not being able to locate a qualified person. This went on until June, when I ended the relationship with that agency and was referred to another one. The new agency sent me a couple of duds before finally getting the right one. It took 4+ years, but today we have an aide who knows her job, is reliable, has a nurturing relationship with Mother, and I only reviewed my trusty Aides Task List with her once—during the initial interview.

Unfortunately, I get no help from my two remaining siblings. Not once have either of them offered to assist in caring for Mother; neither have her grandchildren. The only thing I have received from my siblings is grief. And I'm okay with that because all help is not "good" help. I will not belabor the issue here; however, there has been lots of name calling, false accusations, lying, and deceitfulness on the part of my siblings. Initially, all the animosity took me by surprise, and I was totally

confounded. After a while I realized that their motives were purely selfish and stemmed from their own unresolved issues; it had nothing to do with me. That realization helped me brush their drama aside and continue my journey. But I will say that I am quite envious of those families (one in particular) who developed a plan of action for caring for their parent(s) with shared responsibilities, as they gracefully age in place.

I was busy living my best life, caring for Mother, managing the household, and unwittingly fuming on the inside. I was completely unaware of the unresolved issues that hovered over our relationship. I felt unappreciated, taken for granted, and vilified. There were days when no matter what I did, Mother never saw any good in it. No matter how much love and care I gave, she always saw the dark side. She didn't believe anyone could care for her without something in return. Her self-esteem had been severely damaged during her 50 years of abuse at the hands of her husband. Anytime I tried to get her to enjoy life, she would point out the minutest negative thing and focus on it. I felt as if I was trying to push a Mack truck up a steep hill with the brakes on. I was gradually losing my joyful smile and attitude of gratitude. All this fed into my unwitting, unresolved issue: REJECTION. It took a few therapy sessions to help me realize that as a child and into my adult years I had developed a feeling of being rejected by my mother. She made life choices that, although they were the best decisions for her in the moment, caused me to feel rejected. My therapist helped me to see that many of my life-decisions were attempts to rescue my mother from her abusive environment and when she did not respond in the way I expected I felt

rejected. As her caregiver, this issue rose to the forefront as I attempted to bring joyful experiences into her life, and she responded with negativity. Her responses were literally painful and after a while the pain turned to anger. It took therapy to help me understand that rejection of joy in her life had nothing to do with me. The therapist helped me to realize that my mother's current frame of mind was developed while trying to live and thrive in a racist, patriarchal society while attempting to survive physical and verbal abuse in her home for half a century. Once I was able to get a right perspective on that notion, I became a much better caregiver. I had more patience, more compassion and was able to love her unconditionally.

Twelve years later, I understand that caring for Mother made me realize that life doesn't have to be consumed in huge chunks—it's okay to take it one slice at a time. Now I know that I don't need to juggle so many facets of life. It isn't necessary to have every day filled with appointments, responding to emails, and telephone calls. I don't need to manifest every dream each day. It is perfectly fine to accomplish one thing a day. I do not have to leap tall buildings in a single bound; sometimes it's okay to take the elevator...*I release and I let go!*

Figure 1
Sample Light Housekeeping Duties provided in
Home Care Agency Package

The nursing care plan for Aides and Companions may list light housekeeping as part of the duties to be performed. Occasionally, questions will arise as to what duties are included in LIGHT housekeeping. Please feel free to call our office if you should have any questions or comments about these services. The following items are included in Light Housekeeping duties.

The Bedroom
- Make the client's bed
- Change the client's linens as needed but at least weekly
- Vacuum or sweep the center of the floor without moving furniture
- Dust tops of tables
- Straighten up the room

Living Room/Family Room (only if client is in this room for most of the day)
- Vacuum or sweep the center of the floor without moving furniture
- Dust tops of tables
- Straighten up the room

Bathroom
- Clean up after the client's bath
- Mop floor as needed
- Change towels and wash clothes as requested

Kitchen
- Clean up after meal preparation
- Wash current meal dishes for client only
- Clean up all spills
- Mop floor as needed
- Wipe off counters and stove tops as needed
- Take out trash at least weekly

Miscellaneous
- Client's laundry only, including folding and put laundry away into drawers and/or closets
- Prepare meals for client only

Figure 2
Sample Aides Task List

Week:	COMPLETED				
TASK	MON	TUES	WED	THUR	FRI
BATHROOM (1 day weekly & as needed)					
Clean bathtub including sides & outside					
Clean toilet bowl & rim wipe down seat everyday					
Clean toilet seat, including back & areas behind seat					
Clean top of toilet tank					
Sweep & damp mop the floor					
Clean sink, including bowl & areas on top of vanity					
Clean mirror					
Dust & polish shelves					
BEDROOM					
Change linen 1 day weekly					
Make bed every day					
Change comforter when instructed					
Dust & polish tops of all chests/dressers 1 day weekly					
Dust TV & picture frames 1 day weekly					
Keep drawers neat always					
Vacuum rug twice weekly					
Damp mop hardwood floor 1 day weekly					
HALLWAY					
Vacuum rug twice weekly					
Damp mop hardwood floor 1 day weekly					
LAUNDRY					
Wash dark & light clothes separately as needed					
Fold & put away all laundry as needed					
Keep linen closet neat always					
BATHING					
Bathe (when requested)					
Apply lotion to body and Vaseline to feet always					
LIVING ROOM/DINING ROOM					
Dust & polish furniture 1 day weekly					
Dust TV & picture frames 1 day weekly					
Sweep floors every day					
Vacuum rugs 1 day weekly					
Damp mop hardwood floor 1 day weekly					
Clean mobile stair chair 1 day weekly or as needed					
KITCHEN					
Sweep Floor everyday					
Damp Mop Floor M, W, F					
Clean counters everyday					
Clean stove top everyday					
Wipe down refrigerator 1 day weekly					
Wash dishes everyday					
Put dishes away everyday					
MEAL PREPARATION					
Make food shopping list					
Prepare Lunch meal					
Prepare dinner meal					
TRASH					
Remove trash from bedroom everyday					
Remove trash from bathroom everyday					
Remove trash from kitchen everyday					

Existing caregiving literature has highlighted African American families' positive approach to caregiving and the sense of reward that many experience through caregiving activities despite limited access to health care and other support services and financial hardship. Furthermore, some studies suggest that African American caregivers have less caregiving burden compared to Whites which has been attributed to African American family strengths of valuing elders and the role of religion and spirituality.

Thornton, N., & Hopp, F. P. (2011). "So I Just Took Over": African American Daughters Caregiving for Parents with Heart Failure. Families in Society, 92(2), 211–217. https://doi.org/10.1606/1044-3894.4103

Reflections

A Stitch At A Time

Shimoda Donna Emanuel

My mother is 96 years young with Alzheimer's. She is the second youngest of ten children, six of them were girls. My mother and Aunt Billie (the youngest) took care of the older sisters when they started showing signs of dementia. That was my mother's greatest fear. Here it is.

My cousin said she started showing signs when my dad passed away 20 years ago. I did not notice at the time. Later she started doing strange things like putting chicken in the dishwasher; going to work at the school down the block that she retired from years ago; saying terrible things about people...

My sister lived with her in Queens, and I would go and help sometimes and have her stay with me in Harlem for a couple of days to give my sister a break. I remember my mother made hats as a side business while I was growing up. I used to play with her buttons and her materials. While she was staying with me, I took her to a fiber art class. We worked on a project to honor my dad. She loved it and I saw that she loved sewing buttons. Her art pieces would be full of buttons. At the end of the class, there was an exhibition in a gallery. Everyone's work was behind a glass case. When we got to the reception, her demeanor changed to "I'm an artist!" When I showed her where her art was, she pulled people over to view it. It was amazing to see her transformation. She was

chatting with everyone even though she did not make any sense. By that time her words would come out all jumbled. However, she was very clear that she was the artist.

My sister was showing signs of memory loss and was later diagnosed with breast cancer. It was time for me to take mom. My husband was incredibly supportive. We made room in our condominium and started a new life with mom full time. I now had to juggle doctor appointments with chemo and radiation treatments between my mom and sister. The year of my sister's cancer, I was losing myself. I was burned out and overwhelmed. I was crazy! It was the worst time. I had to call doctors and insurance companies, while also working at my own business. My sister was not as kind as my mom. At times, she would be difficult. My sister's attitude, coupled with her memory loss made supporting her through treatment difficult for me. My sister's treatments lasted a year, and she is now cancer free.

My mother was funny and easy going, so I did not mind having her stay with us, but my work schedule was thrown off. When do I create? I am not getting any work done. How do I create a schedule? It took time but I was able to figure out the best time to do my art. Since mom was getting up later like 1:00 p.m., I would be at my desk by 8:00 a.m. and do my work until 1:00 p.m., get her up, and the rest of the day was taking care of her when I did not have the aide. That worked wonderfully.

Mom would do funny things and I would take photos and kept notes for a future book. I started posting things she would do on

Facebook and Instagram. Some of my friends that were going through the same thing, loved the stories.

Her favorite place was the kitchen, so, I kept a box of "toys" there for her to go through. The box would have buttons, fabric, dominos, magazines, puzzle pieces. She was very neat and organized. There were many times I would walk in the kitchen and see some of these items lined up on the kitchen counter. Or I would lift a lid off a pan I was getting ready to use and see items in there. I would laugh and take a photo.

I was planning on mom staying with me until she passes but that was not the Higher Power's plan. She fell, fractured her hip, had surgery, and went to rehab. During that time, I realized that it would be best for her to be in a nursing home. It is best for her health, my health, and my relationship with my husband. Taking care of her had taken a toll on me. I was so busy taking loving care of her and my sister (remember her?) that I was neglecting myself.

I visit mom at least twice a week. I still want her to come home when I see her, but I am now able to take care of my health, travel with my husband, and recharge my batteries.

Reflections

Finding My Way Home

Kumea Shorter-Gooden

My Mom and I were never very close. We loved each other. We rarely fought. But we weren't close.

I was the independent middle child who moved away and eventually lived on the other coast—for more than a quarter of a century. Mom and I didn't talk much by phone. Hardly ever about personal, revealing things. She was never my confidante. And the time zone difference and the lack of cell phones back in the day cemented a pattern of limited communication. We saw each other two or three times a year and were never estranged or out of touch, but we were never close.

I'm a psychologist, so I'll offer my psych assessment: Mom was an incredibly gifted first-grade teacher who connected with little ones far better than she did with adults. I tend toward counter-dependence—to think I'm self-sufficient and not in need of anyone's support or help. As you can guess, these patterns didn't help our relationship.

As I got older, married, and had a child, I found myself angry at her—off and on—for not "getting me" and for not giving me what I needed—even as I pushed back on the notion that I needed anything. I didn't have the courage to share any of this with her and didn't feel that she would understand or be able to handle it. So, a lot went unsaid.

After about 15 years in California, when our daughter was in high school, I began talking with my husband about moving back home to DC. We had close friends in California, but no family there—all of my family was in DC. My parents had divorced when my two siblings and I were in our 20s, and my father had died suddenly a few years later. Mom was living alone, doing well—she even had a long-term boyfriend whom we all loved, but she was aging, nonetheless. My older brother and younger sister and their spouses were all in the DC area, and I felt a strong calling to go home—to spend much more time with my siblings, cousins, and remaining elders; to be available to Mom; and in some existential way, to return to my birthplace and finish my life there.

The plan fell into place when our daughter Adia was launched and living in Chicago, and I snagged a job in the DC area—my return-home ticket!

Mom was 85 at the time and doing fairly well…. considering. She lived alone in a condo, read *The Washington Post* every morning, enjoyed going to the theater, and still could show up like the woman who'd been named "Best Dressed" as a Howard University student back in 1947. She cooked simple meals and handled her own laundry. However, she'd had to stop driving a few years prior because of problems with her eyesight. That also had meant giving up tutoring in an afterschool program, which she'd been doing since she'd retired as a teacher. Working with children was the one thing—other than her three children and two grandchildren—that buoyed her and gave her a reason to get up every

morning. And most devastating was the fact that her long-time boyfriend, the love of her life, had passed about five years prior.

So, it was a good time for me to show up. All three of her children were now in reach. She and I settled into a pattern of daily brief phone calls and Sunday visits, usually with an outing to the supermarket, often followed by Mom cooking and us eating dinner together. Or we'd go with my sister to see a movie or to a restaurant or jazz concert.

This was a soothing cadence for me. I liked being part of the rhythm of Mom's life, the dailyness of it all. Sitting with her in doctors' waiting rooms. Meeting her physicians and helping her to make sense of their concerns and recommendations. Knowing exactly what to buy for her from the grocery store: "three bananas, two partially green."

We still didn't talk about deep, personal things, and Mom seemed ill-at-ease when asking about my job and my work. She'd drive me crazy sometimes with her incessant nutritional advice: "No raisins in your oatmeal? Why not? It's so much better that way. You've got to try it. Cook them with the oats……" And her constant urging when I was dining at her home, for me to eat more. (Not at all what *my* doctor was advising!) One day I told her she was like a drug-pusher and I threatened that, if she didn't stop, I'd have to cease eating with her altogether.

Mom was lonely and at least mildly depressed. To my surprise, she agreed to my suggestion that she talk with a psychiatrist. I was hoping he'd recommend anti-depressants, but he didn't think she needed them. She enjoyed talking with him, telling her life's story, but after four

sessions, she decided she'd shared all there was, and there was no need to return.

My sister and I began handling her finances when we realized that she was no longer on top of paying bills, and we were able to convince her to have someone come in and clean her place periodically. For a Depression-era woman, who saved and recycled and reused long before it was fashionable, this was a big concession!

One wintry day, when Mom was 89, my sister and I began talking about finding someone to come in to spend time with Mom several hours each week—a companion to help with the loneliness. A few days later, Mom fell and broke her hip. While hospitalized and recovering from the hip surgery, Mom had a stroke. She was delirious. It was horrifying! She finally was moved to rehab, but Mom never mastered walking again. Bound to a wheelchair, she never saw the inside of her condo again.

Mom became more and more depressed and withdrawn, and though she was lucid at times—lucid enough to know how awful things had become—dementia was making its way. She didn't know how old she was. She'd say she was 100. When we spoke of her home, she referred to the family home that she'd grown up in, which she'd left when she was 22. The loss of mobility and memory and home was acute and devastating for her.... and us three children.

We transitioned Mom from rehab to skilled nursing and then several months later to assisted living in a small home. I visited her almost every day—before or after work—and on weekends. My siblings were present, too, but my sister was caring for a husband who was

increasingly ill and disabled, and my brother had moved to the far-flung suburbs. I was juggling a demanding and difficult position as a university administrator and struggling to stay afloat. I realize now that I was in crisis mode and on autopilot for many months. I cried only once, when I realized Mom wasn't going to walk again. But mostly there wasn't time or space to feel or to reflect on my feelings. It was all about what I could do to make Mom more comfortable, to ensure she was being treated well, to advocate forcefully (which was definitely needed at times!), to try to brighten her day, to remind her she was loved, to elicit a faint smile.... Small wins.

And then, a gift. I happily left my job at the university, but my initial plan was to take another position right away. But I didn't. And I was unemployed for the first time ever in my adult life. But it meant I could focus on Mom—spending hours with her, just sitting beside her, trying to amuse her with stories and anecdotes, working hard to engage her. She sometimes understood what was going on, but she spoke very little, answering questions with short, clipped phrases, and hardly initiating any conversation. She'd withdrawn into herself and her connection to the outside world was tenuous and limited. And she was very sad! She seemed utterly heartbroken.

And I was sad, too, sitting beside her every day, holding her hand. But I was very grateful that I was there—day in and day out, and some overnights, too—when she was hospitalized with a second stroke, when she returned to the assisted living facility on hospice care, and then 14

months after her hip fracture, when my sister and I held her hand as she took her very last breath.

My sojourn with Mom was reparative for me. I think it softened me and taught me a lot about love, and particularly what it means to love unconditionally. I mourned my mother's passing, but I was at peace, and I knew she finally was. I moved on with my life—remembering wistfully, celebrating her, working to honor her legacy, feeling sadness at times, but not overwhelmed.

I feel incredibly blessed by Mom's life and by the opportunity to spend her last five years with her. I can't imagine what it would be like for me emotionally if I hadn't returned to DC. It was so important, I believe, for both Mom and me that I found my way home.

Family caregivers generally provide this support without a formal assessment of their needs or the needs of the person receiving support. That means they may have to take on tasks they do not know how to do, did not expect to have to do, or do not feel comfortable doing. They often have limited access to training or assistance that could enable success.

2022 National Strategy to Support Family Caregivers. The Recognize, Assist, Include, Support, and Engage (RAISE) Act Family Caregiving Advisory Council & The Advisory Council to Support Grandparents Raising Grandchildren. 2022

Reflections

Morning Meditations
Kim El

Words, Whispers, Prayers.
Is anyone there?
I speak to God
while sounds & syllables dissipate in the air.
Is anybody there?
I reach out to you
with open palms to the skies
for answers to my "why's"
as my inner child cries
in silence
my heart is bent but not broken.
Life got in the way of living
so now i'm chokin'
and gasping for air.
Is there anyone there?
Please tell me God
am I doomed to repeat the pains of life
in lessons from a karma debt?
I'll wait for answers to my prayers
I trust that it is soon
because it's been nights since I slept.

From the poetry book, "Straightening Combs and Other Things That Changed My Life" by Kim El Copyright 2014

Reflections

His PLAN, Her JOURNEY, My PROMISE
E. Bonita Mitchell

Little did I know that most of my childhood and early adulthood was just a priming ground for the PLAN that I would eventually be charged to do. I am the youngest of three children born to Eula Mae Keels and Dave Mitchell. Elizabeth "Bunni" Mitchell that is me, often referred to as a mama's girl and grandma's knee baby (because every time grown folks talked about something, I was parked on the floor beside the talker's knee— just plain nosey). I kept my mouth shut and ears open, and I learned a lot!

My mother was raised in Seneca, SC, and she was the second oldest out of twelve children. Her mother, lovingly called Big Mamma was the first caregiver that I can remember. In the early '60s through the early '70s, I would always accompany my mother on a trip to Greenville, SC to care for her aging parents. They had a beautiful ranch-styled house with chickens and one pig. I would often wonder why mommy was the only sibling that came down to care for Big Mamma and granddaddy on a regular basis. When I became older, I learned that everyone is not suited to do the same thing in this life. In this case that chore landed in my mother's lap along with her younger brother, James. Together they would work out a plan to take care of their aging parents with love and dignity; and I was there every step of the way, seeing, hearing, watching everything that took place, but not understanding that these events were life lessons on which I would one day depend.

My grandmother developed Alzheimer's in the mid- to late-60s. I can remember the last time my mother went down south and when she came back home, she made the announcement that Big Mamma and granddaddy would be

moving to DC. I was so happy until I learned that meant they would live with us. You see, my granddaddy was a very well-known Southern minister, Reverend Dr. Curtis Matthew David Keels, so that meant that when they came to live with us, it would be a whole new set of rules and ethics that we youngsters had to follow. It was a challenge for me, but I soon fell into line and did as I was told. As time went by, Big Mamma was placed in a nursing home because it became harder for mom to work, take care of her family and home and care for her father. I watched my mother lovingly and patiently take care of both her parents until they both succumbed to their diseases: Big Mamma of Alzheimer's and granddaddy from cancer.

I lost my stepdad in the early '80s but before he died, he asked my brother to stay very close to my mother and to watch out for her because my dad felt that she was going to be just like her mother, meaning she would one day have Alzheimer's, and eventually she did. By that time, I was the last child living at home. My father did not want me to move; he did not think it was proper for a young lady to move out of her home without getting married, but he respected that times had changed and soon gave me his infamous nod of approval. I was anxious and excited about moving on my own. I was packing my boxes and I had already decided that me and my best childhood girlfriend would be roommates. I was ready to conquer the world. And then mommy's JOURNEY began and the PLAN kicked in. My brother came to me and asked me not to move because mommy was starting to forget, her memory was failing, and she would need help around the house. I did not skip a beat, I did not give it a second thought, I just looked at him and said, "Okay, big brother. Okay." I never could say no to my brother.

Even though it was just me and mommy in the house, we would always cook together like we were having company. One day while cleaning greens, she

turned to me and asked, "Do you think you would wanna take care of me in my old age if I needed you?" I looked into her eyes and said, "Mommy, for all that you sacrificed for the three of us and your family, I would take care of you in a heartbeat with no problems and no second thoughts, and that's the deal and PROMISE that I want to make with you right now. I love you, mommy, and thanks for showing me real love." I got up, walked over to the sink to hug and kiss her and whispered in her ear, "So stop worrying. Stop worrying. I'm here for the long haul—I got your back." You see, she knew she was forgetting, and she was scared.

At that moment and for the next 17 years I became my mother's primary caregiver. I took care of every aspect of her life, and every day I reminded myself that my mother did the same thing for the three of us—at the same time. And she also housed every one of her sisters as they made their way from the South to whatever dreams they were chasing. They all made our home a vacation destination. Those siblings had a close bond that was never broken except by death, and that behavior and example would become the gold standard for my immediate family. Did I tell you that they were stair-step children except for the last three (the twins and the last-born boy)? They almost died in that order, too, give or take a couple of years. We even had to divide family members to attend same day funerals for three of them. Every female child died from Alzheimer's and or dementia-related issues.

My mother had always been a mild-mannered woman, very patient but stern. She did not believe in having a lot of chaos in her home, just a loving home headed by a loving husband and father, and God at the helm. Through the entire course of my mother's disease, her personality never changed. She continued to be mild mannered and patient. Of course, other physical attributes changed with her like losing her short-term memory, not being able to bathe herself, feed

herself, sometimes not knowing where she was, and near the end, not being able to speak. All these physical changes really did not upset me. The most important thing in my mind was that she felt loved, protected, and had an excellent quality of life—and that I would remain a woman of my word and follow through with my deal and PROMISE.

I became absorbed in reading everything I could get my hands on regarding Alzheimer's and dementia, all while still working a full-time job. And with that course of action, I really didn't have time to be sad. I didn't have the luxury of pitying myself or my mother. I had a job to do, and I had to equip myself the best way I could—with book knowledge and my faith in God, while taking care of the one thing that I loved most in this world. Every day, I prayed to God that He would make me ready for my mother's eventual death, because until then I could not imagine being in this world without her. He had a PLAN, and He did more than make me ready. He gave me every single tool that I needed to take care of his child Eula Mae. I wanted to be a good steward over every tool and gift given to me so, I let Him guide me. We were in good hands!

I soon found a daycare for my mother while I worked every day. This worked out great for both of us. It kept her active, engaged, and busy, and it also eased my mind and my worries. This went on until my body became extremely tired. It had taken a beating, and I no longer could work full-time and take care of mommy. So, I retired early and came home to finish/execute my PROMISE. Even though I had an older sister and brother, in the very beginning they were not a lot of help, and I didn't mind. I didn't miss it, and I didn't care because my focus was strictly on my mother, but after about five years I realized that they could be doing more. It was a bit of a tug of war trying to get them to understand what I was going through and what their mother was going through. It was just extra stress on me to have to tell them sometimes to help me. Sometimes I

would even cry myself to sleep wondering why they didn't seem to love their mother the way I loved her. Eventually I had an epiphany. If God loved and accepted me just the way I was then I should do the same for my sister and my brother and with that new knowledge all my stress went away. And believe it or not my sister and brother came around and they started helping more. They would buy some of her nutritional needs like Ensure, food bars and things that she loved like fruits, pecan bars, and prunes and also some of her personal hygiene items. That was a real big help for me. This meant I didn't have to find a babysitter just to run to the store to pick up things for my mother. I was truly grateful. I learned that comprehensive understanding and/or enlightenment is not reached at the same time for everyone.

I made another PROMISE to my mom as time went by, I promised her that I would keep her in her home and familiar surroundings for as long as I could keep her safe. But the time did come when I could not keep her safe. You see, for many years I carried my mother up and down thirteen steps from living room to bedroom and lifted her in and out of bed and that monster of a bathtub. Pretty soon my knees wore out, and I could no longer take care of her safely. Her doctor would say every month for ten years, "You are doing the work of three shift nurses and three health care aides. Let me place your mother in a nice nursing home." I said "No," I have a promise to keep! While my mother was in rehab for hip replacement therapy, that same doctor kept her there so long that every day I asked "When is my mother coming home? Somebody better tell me something or else!" She finally said, "I held your mother here until a permanent room became available." To my surprise, the doctor was also a prominent board member at the hospital as well as the nursing home where mommy rehabbed. Wow. He still performs miracles, taking little to make much.

I have always listened to that quiet voice in my spirit, and I knew this was part of His PLAN.

Once mommy was placed in the nursing home, I became so lonely without her. I did have a plan for myself so I would visit her EVERY day, reading the newspaper, the Bible and styling her hair and singing her favorite hymns and gospels. We often had praise service and ended the day with a mild massage, a warm wipe down, and of course our nightly prayer. Mommy went to be with the Lord on a cold Wednesday night. My heart and mind were prepared. The nurse asked if I wanted to come to the nursing home to see her one last time while she was still warm; I declined. I had just prayed with mommy that day and gave her roses while she could smell them. All I could do after receiving the phone call that she had passed was run into an empty room and thank God for keeping His promises and for making me ready for her departure. I think I praised Him for an hour then returned to my bedroom where I fell into my husband's arms and finally had a good cry. My siblings went to see her one last time and then came to be with me. I took comfort in sharing this special event with them—it drew us closer together.

One of the most valuable lessons that I learned on this journey was to be more patient, to literally try to visualize myself as the other person and not just the person that I was caring for, but also for surrounding members of my family and close friends. It has helped me tremendously by causing me to process what I am hearing before I react. I do not think I would have done anything differently except to stay more socially connected.

I remain grateful for all the resources and tools that assisted me on this journey, like AARP Wandering/ID program, DC Department on Aging, The Downtown Cloister Program (for adult daycare), my neighbors who always kept me and my mother in their hearts, and last but not least, the Greater First

Baptist Church of Mount Pleasant Plains (Washington, DC) who kept my family in prayer.

My advice to others who are experiencing caregiving is to educate yourself with as much information as you can and to use and rely on other professional people and institutions to help you facilitate a plan of action. Most importantly, take care of yourself first: take breaks, use respite care for your loved one, and stay healthy, do not forego your health. It has been a transforming journey; I have grown in a number of ways: my faith walk is stronger, my love for others has expanded, and my love of self has a whole new meaning. If I had to do it again, I would. Rest in peace, mom. I will see you when I get there!

Reflections

_____
_____
_____
_____
_____
_____
_____
_____
_____
_____
_____
_____
_____
_____
_____
_____
_____
_____
_____
_____
_____

My Journey with Mama
Belinda Robinson Stanford

Becoming the primary caregiver for my 86-year-old Mom, Beatrice Robinson, resulted after months of persuasion. Mama had lived alone for four years after the death of my Daddy (her husband of 64 years). Mama reluctantly agreed to move in and live with me in November 2006.

Mama was born in Sunflower County, Mississippi. She and Daddy met there and married. They were part of the Great Migration to Chicago. She found employment as a maintenance supervisor at Penn Central Railroad, now Amtrak. She worked there for 42 years! After living in Chicago for a few years, Mama and Daddy bought property in Robbins, IL, built a home, and lived there for over 50 years.

My mother was the oldest of five siblings. She was their encouragement and second mom. Her love for her entire family was evident in her incredible generosity and the way that she shared her deep wisdom freely. Her radiant smile could light up a room.

My parents had two daughters. I'm the oldest, and my mom has been my best friend since birth. We shopped and baked together, traveled together, and went to church together.

When she moved in with me, Mama enjoyed cleaning her bathroom, dusting her bedroom, cooking meals, and washing and folding her own laundry. Mama's health began to decline in 2009. She had severe

osteoporosis in her back and knees and required the use of a rollator (walker). She was still determined to continue her activities, sitting and resting as needed along the way.

In addition to visiting a primary care physician for quarterly wellness checkups, Mama needed several specialty physicians. Due to heart valve issues, a cardiologist prescribed medication for heart palpitations. He called Mama's heart "noisy" but sturdy! Mama also wore glasses and her ophthalmologist whom we visited yearly would sing "Mrs. Robinson" from the movie *The Graduate* at each office visit. After two cataract surgeries, dry eye issues and the diagnosis of macular degeneration, we started to hear "Mrs. Robinson" more frequently.

Mama also needed a podiatrist for foot and toenail care. She was not diabetic, but her toenails were difficult to cut. She met with an Eye, Nose, Throat (ENT) physician twice a year due to heavy ear wax build-up. Mama required "tubes" for ear drainage.

Mama did not wear dentures. Her teeth (only three molars missing!) were straight and strong. Her dentist would send her flowers on her birthday; she was his oldest patient.

Mama needed those strong teeth because she loved to eat. Breakfast was her favorite meal, especially if there was bacon, soft-scrambled eggs, toast with butter and strawberry jam, pancakes and sausages with syrup, coffee with cream and sugar or tea with two teaspoons of sugar.

Her favorite dinner was fried chicken wings, catfish, sugared carrots, mashed potatoes, dinner rolls, fresh green beans, white potatoes

simmered with onions, ham cubes, and pimento for color. Mama liked a pretty plate of food! If it didn't look right, she wouldn't eat it. And she always wanted a slice of pound cake for dessert.

Mama was also very particular about her appearance. At 90 years old she was tinting her hair black. She didn't like grey or white hair. Her attire was always lady-like. Her church outfit was a suit with matching hat, gloves, and scarf.

During these years of many doctors' appointments and declining physical health, I realized that I needed HELP! I needed a secretary to keep up with the doctor's visits. A giant wall calendar was my good friend. But I didn't ask for assistance.

But after my total knee replacement surgery in 2016, I finally began searching for help. Catholic Charities was very helpful and after a home visit Mama was assigned a Home Health Aide who came three times a week for four hours a day.

Mama initially resisted the idea, saying she didn't need anyone to take care of her. I had to let Mama know that *I* needed help. *I* couldn't do it all, and *I* needed help to care for her. Eventually Mama agreed because she wanted to help me.

Well, Mama *loved* Geri, our Home Health Aide. Geri was a very special person who also cared for her 90-year-old Mom. With Geri, it was like having another me. She arrived early in the morning, and she would get Mama out of bed, showered and dressed. Geri would make up the bed or change and wash the linen, clean the bathroom, fix breakfast, and

assist in feeding Mama. She was a companion for Mama if I had a doctor's appointment or needed to run errands.

As Mama's physical health declined, she also began experiencing cognitive deterioration. For example, Mama, who was a perfectionist and had long been proud of her handwriting, could no longer write legibly and would become frustrated and ball up the piece of paper when her penmanship wasn't perfect. Mama also had increasing difficulty in daily functions: bathing, dressing herself, brushing her teeth, and combing her hair. Mama's osteoporosis often caused new fractures including right foot, left heel, right hip, and right thigh. Her mobility was on the decline. Already using a rollator, Mama's difficulty transferring from the bed to the wheelchair meant she needed a Sit to Stand Lift.

But despite it all, Mama still loved to attend Sunday morning worship services at church. Still dressed in her church outfit and polished nails, and at 95+ years old there was not a noticeable strand of gray hair on her head. She visited the beauty salon often to get her Black Rinse. Yet getting Mama to church and the beauty salon without assistance was not easy for me. Much prayer and God gave me the strength. And seeing how meaningful it was for Mama to see her friends at church made it all worthwhile for me.

In November 2019, after 13 years of caring for Mama, she was placed in home hospice care. In February 2020, Mama's tibia was fractured. Due to her insurance policy, Mama was admitted to the hospital for care of the fracture but could not be admitted as a hospice care patient. There is a difference between Original Medicare and

Hospice Medicare. After being admitted to the hospital for a three-night stay, Mama became a resident at a nursing rehabilitation facility to receive physical therapy because she could no longer stand.

The COVID-19 global pandemic hit the US in March 2020 and because of the pandemic, the nursing facility stopped physical therapy and visits from family members. Mama was only receiving help in group settings. Not being able to visit my 99-year-old mother, who because of her dementia could not understand it all, was very difficult for me. There are no words to express how painful it was to not be able to rescue her immediately.

The most heartbreaking part of Mama being in the nursing facility is that she was there for her 100th birthday. I had spent months working with her four grandchildren to plan an amazing celebration. And Mama liked a party! It was so sad to only be able to see and celebrate her through a glass window because of COVID. After all Mama had lived through in her 100 years, it seemed unfair that celebrating her centennial was snatched from her and us. I was so upset and distressed that day that I ended up calling my doctor and being prescribed medication.

After much prayer, I called the hospice, had my mom reinstated for Hospice Medicare, and brought her back home with me. Lord knows I didn't know what I was going to do with my mother on my own. But I knew I would love her until death!

Hospice Care was a God send! Hospice supplied all the needed medical equipment, including a hospital bed and oxygen. A Hoyer lift was provided. At first, I was terrified of that machine. The RN provided

instructions and eventually I became a pro! Mama was very happy to be home and cooperated well with all the hospice staff.

With the further decline of mobility came more cognitive decline. Simple tasks caused frustration, like folding a paper napkin, which she'd previously done with ease. Mama would get upset when she couldn't complete tasks. My solution was to change tasks and either take a nap or watch cartoons (the news was stressful, too!) when frustrations arose.

A previously very talkative Mama became more silent. She had loved to talk to her church friends and would always say "I'm blessed" after each conversation. Soon, it took too much energy to talk, and conversations became very short.

During the COVID pandemic our home health aide Geri couldn't provide services and the Hospice Care was limited. Though we couldn't have family members visit us inside our condo, they did visit with us from the parking lot while Mama and I stayed on the balcony upstairs. My only sibling, a younger sister, would visit and help, when possible, though she lives in a neighboring state.

Some days Mama would sit and look at the sky and say how beautiful it was and ask me not to "take it away." She was so calm and peaceful, just enjoying the view.

Mama and I shared everything, and when it became necessary, I was honored to bathe, cook, dress, take her to appointments, and manage her affairs. I learned that I was stronger physically, mentally, and spiritually due to being Mama's daughter. But sometimes to a fault. For example, my mom was always determined to do her best. She used to say,

"nothing beats a failure but a try." Her neurologist called her "dangerously independent," so much so that we had to put safety alarms on the guardrails on her bed. It kept me nervous 24/7, not knowing if she might fall out of the bed or try to get out of her wheelchair. I now realize that I'm dangerously independent, too. But I'm learning.

I've always had the mindset that "God will supply who and what you need, when you need it." That was true as I cared for Mama. Many resources were helpful on this journey with Mama. I learned that you must share your needs. I learned not to expect help from everyone, but I was surprised by what and how help was provided.

My mom, Beatrice Robinson passed away at 101 years old, exactly one week after a beautiful Mother's Day filled with smiles, kisses, and hugs. Surrounded by family and friends at home, Mama slipped away on Sunday, May 16, 2021.

Reflections

Loving Her in Her Second Childhood
Kim El

In 2016, I went on a trip to Ghana, West Africa with my students. One of the things I learned while I was there was how aging parents and elders were treated in their families. There is an African proverb that says, "She who has cared for me when I had no teeth and could not walk, I will now care for her when she has no teeth and cannot walk." During that week in Ghana, we stayed in Jukwa, a small village with lots of history and hospitality. I noticed that there were many extended families with an elder living in the household. This cultural reality was very enlightening and created a new perception on my views of aging. On my flight back I thought about my awesome experience in Ghana and the beautiful African customs/rituals that honor the seniors in their community.

Fast forward to Pittsburgh, PA. It is January 3, 2021. My 82-year-old mother has a deep brain stroke. It was a blessing that she survived despite some muscle paralysis on her left side. Mom went from healing in the hospital to a rehabilitation facility. She was there for a month. All of this happened during the continuation of the 2020 COVID-19 Pandemic. Mom's illness had a devasting effect on her life and changed the dynamics of our family. I am the oldest of Mom's three daughters and we agreed that mom was *not* going into a nursing home. The COVID vaccine had just came out and there were too many stories of elders

dying in nursing homes from the COVID virus. We decided that we would take turns caring for her.

When Mom came back to her apartment in February her doctors told us that she needed 24-hour care. Mom could not walk or stand without a walker. Stability and balance were challenging. Using the toilet required someone to help her. She needed assistance to get dressed and put on her shoes. Despite her ability to feed herself, she had a choking hazard due to some throat paralysis. My sisters and I took turns bathing her and getting her in and out of bed. Mom was totally dependent on us.

Who is our mom? Her name is Joan. She was born on March 8, 1939, in Pittsburgh, PA in the historic Hill District. Before her stroke, Mom was a retired Licensed Practical Nurse who loved to crochet, read murder mysteries, cook, smoke cigarettes and do crossword puzzles. Now, she lives in a three-room senior citizens apartment complex. Her world revolves around her daughters and their families. She has five grandchildren and seven great-grandchildren. Generosity and kindness are within Mom's spirit. But her language is often unfiltered and sprinkled with cuss words every now and then. When she had her stroke, she tried to cuss, but her speech was slurred so it didn't have the same effect. As her speech improved, so did her cussing. This is how we knew she was getting better! Mom smoked almost two packs of cigarettes a day and often told us that she was a cigarette addict. Her doctor said the cigarettes were a major factor in her having a stroke.

Since it was necessary for Mom to have around the clock care, I called the Area Agencies on Aging, googled resources on the internet, and

contacted Mom's patient advocate. Unfortunately, we were having a hard time finding a nurse or home aide to assist her/us because of Mom's insurance. I was told by her patient advocate that Mom was eligible for Medicaid and through them more resources for her would be available. While we were waiting for Medicaid and researching home aide assistance, I moved in with Mom. It was February 2021 and during this time the senior citizens in Mom's building were offered free COVID vaccines. We were glad that Mom received both vaccinations. My sisters and I were also vaccinated.

In my other life, outside of being mom's caregiver, I am a 62-year-old playwright on disability. I have a rare condition, laryngospasm, which sometimes makes it difficult for me to breathe. Being a caregiver and having my own health issues are very challenging for me but not impossible. When mom had her stroke, I was in the process of waiting to sign a lease for a new apartment for myself and things have shifted a bit. Staying at Mom's apartment is now my new normal.

Caregiving is indeed a sacrifice of time, work, and personal responsibilities for myself and my siblings. My sister Deb is a Registered Nurse with medical skills and knowledge that are helpful with Mom's care. However, Deb's 9-to-5 nursing job makes her availability limited. Cheryl is our youngest sister who is a great cook and provides awesome homecooked meals, light housekeeping and runs grocery errands. She is a professional actress and makeup artist. Cheryl balances her caregiving time between rehearsals and performances. Although my sisters and I take turns caring for Mom, I am her primary caregiver. This includes

being her medical advocate, managing finances and bills, monitoring medicine, bathing, cooking, dressing, and keeping her spiritually and emotionally lifted. Mom's patient advocate connected me with a Pennsylvania Waivers program, and I am financially compensated for some of the hours spent taking care of our beloved mother. Despite our busy lifestyles, we all feel love with a powerful responsibility and obligation to help our Mother heal. I believe this is what families should do.

In April 2021 I signed the lease to my new apartment and moved my furniture in. This caregiving journey began in the winter and it is now the hot summer of August. I am still here taking care of and living with Mom Monday thru Friday until we can find another arrangement. Basically, I only spend time in my new apartment on the weekends. However, after a month of caring for our mother, I realized that *self-care* was just as important as being a *caregiver*. At first, I felt guilty about taking time out for myself. But my mind concluded that if something were to happen to me, who would provide the additional care for our mother? Self-care is not being selfish. I believe it is a much-needed ingredient for a successful caregiving experience. Fortunately, we were able to get homecare aides to rotate caregiving for Mom on the weekends. I decided that the weekends at my new apartment would be my much-needed respite and time to rejuvenate.

If there is any worse part of being Mom's caregiver, it is watching her transition from a strong African American family matriarch to a sometimes depressed, dependent patient. It hurts my heart to see the

look on her face when she is not able to walk to the stove to cook or turn a page in a book. But even witnessing the worse part, I am grateful for the opportunity to care for her in her time of need.

Elder care can be quite demanding and often overwhelming with stressful days. As I mentioned earlier, I have health issues and there are some days when I just want to lay down and get uninterrupted rest. But I can't. Mom will ring her bell to use the toilet or maybe she has a doctor's appointment on that day. When my sisters or the home aides are not available, I push myself to persevere. I also experience helplessness and some mild depression knowing that there is not much I can do to change Mom's health situation. Overall, my transition from being the "child" into parenting my parent has its mixture of good and not so good times.

One of the good things for me about caregiving is talking with Mom while doing tasks with her. There is another African proverb that says, "When an elder dies, a library burns to the ground." Older people like to tell stories about their life experiences. Most of the time people don't slow down to listen to them. When I say people, I mean me. I have learned that her stories are valuable gems to be passed down from generation to generation. Spending long hours with Mom allowed me to hear her stories about her youth and family members I have never heard her talk about. It is interesting learning about her/my family history. In turn, I share my life stories of college days and crazy antics with her over cups of coffee and laughter. Since I became her caregiver, our close mother-daughter bond has become even closer. For every overwhelming day, there would be three or more days of a positive experience with her.

I also emphasize the need for her to have trust in restoration of her health. It makes me smile when she tells people she is a stroke "survivor" and not a stroke "victim."

Other good things about caregiving is that we get to give Mom back all the love, nurturing, and boo boos that she kissed when we were growing up. Everything I have done, am doing and will continue to do for my mother is exactly what she did for me when I was a child. She changed my diapers, fed me, protected me, and took care of me when I was sick. It all comes back full circle. Prior to her stroke, Mom didn't have many visitors. Now her face lights up when she is surrounded by family and friends. She also has become cyber savvy. Mom watches cooking shows on the internet and listens to her murder mysteries on audio books through her tablet. "Alexis, resume Audible" is usually the last thing I hear before she goes to sleep. We believe that it is necessary for Mom to maintain a sense of security, spirituality, emotional stability, and some independence while she is rehabilitating from her illness. Our goal is to make sure that this stroke has not totally disrupted her quality of life.

My advice to caregivers of loved ones are:
- Be Patient. Remember that this is the first time for them being cared for. Confirm from doctors and specialists how much care is needed.
- Discuss home care with other family members.
- Look for home care services that offer medical and/or personal care.
- Research financial support. Check out Medicare Waivers that

pay caregivers. Find Ready-Made Meal Services (Meals On Wheels, Mom's Meals)

- When things get overwhelming, call for extra help.
- Utilize a Patient Advocate for medical questions and concerns.
- You can't do everything by yourself. Share the responsibilities to avoid burnout. Take time out for yourself without feeling guilty.
- Laugh at the little things that go wrong. Laughter is very healing.

It was a blessing for me to experience Ghana and witness this familial culture in the Motherland. I believe that my mindset about being a caregiver for mom may be slightly different from my sisters because of this. I will end my story with the word "Ubuntu." It is a Nguni Bantu expression that means, "I am who I am because you are who you are." I am my mother's child. I am grateful to be in her life to help her navigate through the trials and tribulations of her stroke. Peace and Blessings to all the caregivers who really care.

Reflections

_____
_____
_____
_____
_____
_____
_____
_____
_____
_____
_____
_____
_____
_____
_____
_____
_____
_____
_____
_____
_____

The Things No One Told Me

Lesa Moore

No one told me that this would be the beginning of the end. The end of your earthly existence and the beginning of your eternal existence.

No one told me how scared it would be to enter your bedroom not knowing what to expect and also how brave I would feel the moment you would look me in my eyes.

No one told me how mentally exhausting this would be. Always focusing on what's next.

No one told me about that one moment in time when it would hit me that you wouldn't get better and how helpless I would feel.

No one told me that the weekly pill containers would be a godsend.

No one told me that the saying "It takes a village" would mean so much more to me now.

No one told me that I would have a new appreciation for a hospital bed and bed pads.

No one told me I would end up feeding you, changing you and bathing you like a baby.

No one told me how the softest touch could be so painful to you and when you would wince, so would I.

No one told me you would forget who I was.

No one told me that your mind would be stuck at the age of 14.

No one told me I would forever remember how soft your skin was and how that memory brings me so much comfort.

No one told me how honored I would feel to take care of you.

No one told me you would ask me if you were dying and that it was okay because God has your room ready.

No one has to tell me that if I had the chance to do it ALL over again, I would do it in a heartbeat.

I LOVE YOU AND MISS YOU. UNTIL WE MEET AGAIN MY PRECIOUS GRANDMA.

African Americans are more often in a high intensity care situation – provides 31.2 hours of care weekly, helps with 2.1 ADLs, 4.7 IADLs and medical/nursing tasks.

Caregiving in the U.S. - Fact Sheet - The "Typical" African American Caregiver, National Alliance for Caregiving and AARP. 2020.

Reflections

Caregiving as a Married Couple
Hank and Charlene Davis

We are Hank and Charlene, an African American couple that have been married for over 30 years. Our parental caregiving began for Hank's parents and grandmother over 10 years ago. At that time, we were in our late forties with a son in his late twenties.

Our family roots evolve from Nigeria. The Nigerian family values include a strong tradition of mutual caring and responsibility among the family members. With the responsibilities of our own lives, we knew the importance of respecting our elders and their needs. Oftentimes, I watched my husband, as the eldest son, fulfill the roles of husband, father, and caregiver. We knew the importance of visiting our parents, chatting on the phone, and checking on them as they aged. During conversations with our son, we talked about the obligations we had to our families, even if they did not feel the same way. If we did not take care of our parents, would our son take care of us?

The first caregiving role for us started with Grandmother Bea. She was born in 1927 and worked in a hospital environment until she retired in 1990. Having a sound mind and her independence were of the utmost importance to her. She had four children of which she buried two of them within a year. The two living children, Delores, and Keith lived their own lives and rarely visited their mother. Delores lived 10-15 minutes away and Keith lived on the west coast.

Grandmother Bea was living in a senior's housing complex. We lived close by and became her caregivers. Her needs included banking, grocery shopping, transportation to appointments, light house cleaning, cooking and outings with us.

When she lost her best friend, she needed additional contact with family. She would not call her daughter Delores, but instead called her grandson, Hank. Since Hank traveled internationally for work, Charlene took the role as the primary support person to relieve Hank. There was a gradual decline in her memory as she developed dementia and became paranoid. When her mental faculties began to fail, Charlene and Hank discussed with their Uncle Keith the need for a home health aide. Charlene hired a trusted friend to provide meal preparation, engage Grandmother Bea in light exercise, transportation to the store and companionship 3 days a week. During this time Grandmother Bea's eating habits could be monitored, and someone could socialize with her while we were at work or on travel. We could not enlist any help from Delores because she was providing care for her husband, Harry. Grandmother Bea did not have a relationship with her other grandchildren. We provided care for her for over 10 years.

The only issue we had with Grandmother Bea was that she felt Keith could do no wrong, even though he would not avail himself to take care of his mother. Keith was retired and the executor of her estate. It is difficult to manage your life and that of someone else, too. Others seem to feel the more you do the less they have to. People can be selfish if it does not directly affect them.

As dementia set in, Grandmother Bea's faculties quickly began a downward spiral. She repeatedly wandered away from her apartment and was found outside in the rain wearing only her pajamas. She also thought her apartment had been burglarized. The police were notified of the alleged incidents. We received numerous calls, day or night, regarding her condition and the need for constant monitoring. This became challenging since we both worked. Keith delayed any action until the housing complex threatened to call social services. The policy of the housing complex is to notify social services when the elderly become incapacitated and the caregivers cannot meet the needs of the senior. This was not an assisted living complex or nursing home.

We explained to Keith that he needed to begin taking responsibility for the care of his mother because Hank accepted a position working overseas. Keith immediately finalized the arrangements and moved her to a nursing facility on the west coast. Dementia does not wait until it is convenient. Even though Grandmother Bea wanted her independence, she knew she could not take care of herself.

Overall, the time we spent together talking about family and her life experiences were some of the best memories we have. She always said goodbye by saying Love, Love, Love You. Grandmother Bea passed from COVID-19 in November 2020, one week before her 93rd birthday.

The other parental caregiving role was for Hank's parents, Delores and Harry. Harry was a retired welder who lived with his wife, Delores. Throughout their lives they had issues with alcohol abuse.

Delores worked in finance for over 40 years at the same company until they made her retire. Delores and Harry had a co-dependent relationship. Hank and his two younger brothers had unresolved issues with their parents. The sons felt that their mother put their father before them, and their father prioritized his extended family above his immediate family. Through various conversations with their parents, the sons discussed their feelings and came to a mutual understanding that their parents were in denial. No one is harboring any ill will from the past. Having discussions about their parents was therapeutic. This did not stop them from providing supplemental care in the form of financial support, running errands, visitations, and shopping.

In 2013 Harry started to have health issues and did not follow the doctor's orders. This caused numerous trips to the hospital. Delores was now retired, but tired and requested her eldest son, Hank, to assist with ensuring Harry followed the doctor's orders. Harry chose to do what he wanted to do, even though he knew the consequences.

Delores did not like change. She loved Harry so much she could not manage caring for him. It was difficult watching her inability to complete the simplest paperwork or make decisions, something she usually managed effortlessly. Delores was not able to effectively manage Harry's needs. During a visit to the hospital, Charlene had to fulfill the role of spouse regarding Harry's care.

In 2015, the decision was made that Harry needed to be in an assisted living/long term care facility. He began to tell us about dreams of his ancestors that came to visit him. We enjoyed diverse conversations

with Harry and had the opportunity to spend time with him outside of the facility so he could feel the sun on his face. His death followed a few weeks later in August 2015 at the age of 75. Harry died with a smile on face.

Caregiving for Delores evolved when Harry passed. She became bitter, depressed, and did not want to live. She made it difficult because she would not take any advice on improving her situation due to her grief. Even though she spoke with grief counselors, she did not care about living. We felt there was nothing else we could do but pray. We offered for her to move in with us, but she declined. During our visits, we would take her food but found out she would not eat it. We had to make sure she knew her children and grandchildren loved her. That was not enough to live for.

After a year, Hank's middle brother, Greg, moved in with his mother to provide care. He thought it only fair since we had to provide care for Grandmother Bea. Greg took over her finances and household chores. In January 2017, we moved overseas. Greg had Delores admitted to an assisted living facility. She passed away at the age of 72 from failure to thrive 2 years and 1 day from the anniversary of Harry's death.

As a married couple, we feel in sickness and health also applies to our extended family. We can suggest prayer, patience and attempt to enlist other family members to assist. You must be okay with making the sacrifices or you will harbor anger that will cause you to be stressed and unhappy. There is no burden that God will put on us that we cannot handle. There is not anything we could have done differently because

others did not care as much as we did. If we had it to do all over again, we would fulfill our responsibility of taking care of our parents and grandparents. Having the privilege to care for an elderly relative or our seniors is one that comes with lessons. While being a caregiver is trying and not something everyone is cut out for, its rich rewards cannot truly be defined. We are strong African Americans; it comes from our ancestors and our faith in our God.

[S]tudies show that many [African Americans] feel a better sense of purpose than their caregiver counterparts: "this is what kin do."

Barry J. Jacobs, AARP. Community and Culture Help Black Caregivers Cope With the Challenges of Family Caregiving. 2021
https://www.aarp.org/caregiving/basics/info-2021/african-american-caregivers-cope-better.html

Reflections

What We Hope Never Cracks

Marcia V. Ellis

It was the call that I anticipate hearing but hope that I never do. My sister who was with our mom on her level of the house at around 6:00 in the morning called me on my phone two floors up in our townhouse and said, "Something is wrong with mom." Grabbing my glasses and my phone I got to her level as quickly and safely as possible. Mom and my sister were in her bathroom. Mom was dressed for the day. My sister had bathed, lotioned, powdered, and dressed her, a part of our normal early morning routine. It's something that mom enjoys and that gives us pleasure to do. But here she was seated, slumped on the lid of her toilet and totally unconscious and unresponsive. My sister and I quickly agreed that we should call 911. In the meantime, we called mom's name several times. We stroked her face and used our most endearing terms to get her to respond. Her face was clammy and gray. She was sweating profusely. For several minutes she did not respond. My sister provided information to the EMS staff on the phone as she ran around to collect her DNR (Do-Not-Resuscitate Order) and other documents. I remained with mom, stroking her gently and softly calling her name. I said to my sister, "I think we are losing her." My sister asked, "Do you think we are?" I said simply "yes." Mom was passed out for about 15 minutes. She's had similar episodes before but this one seemed different.

Mom survived her episode, is now thriving and has resumed her leadership position in the family. In fact, after feeling that we might be losing her, in comes the group of EMS people and the voice of one of them calling out to her brought her immediately back to consciousness. I mean, she was all smiles and speaking in whole sentences. Her skin had miraculously returned to its normal luster and beauty, and she engaged them and my sister and me as though nothing ever happened. My sister and I looked at one another in shock, realizing that those who came to help mom probably now needed to help us instead!

Mom is 98 years old. To look at her, you wouldn't think that she is. She's a beautiful woman who is usually very present mentally and vibrant. And she is very conscious about her hygiene and her style. She loves looking well put together. But this past year and a half of COVID, we have noticed her mental and physical decline. Still, she amazes us most times.

We're blessed to be a close family of seven siblings. Our father and his namesake, our oldest brother, are Ancestors. Two siblings live in Miami but remain central to mom's health and well-being. Then there are lots of grands and great grands, now young adults (and a couple of great, great grands). The siblings have a group text and then we have a larger family text that includes the grands and the older great grands. Through those texts we communicate from early morning through the end of the day, virtually celebrating these days our family milestones and other news. That news includes news of and from mom. Together, we form mom's circle of love and care. My siblings and I, though, form her primary

caregiving circle. From the time that mom came back to live with me in the townhouse that we originally co-owned, we put in place a very tight system for her care. It is a system that had to consider our own very busy lives with our jobs, our support for our adult children and their little ones, close friends, and our own care as aging seniors with our own health needs and challenges.

Our system works well most times. But we've learned that even though there are several of us, it is never enough. Before COVID, we'd often hire or solicit the help of neighbors and friends who would help us with mom's care and comfort. Mostly, they provided companionship, transportation, and company to church or other outings when we were not available. At that time, she was also active in our local Senior Center where she'd go twice a week on a bus that would pick her up and bring her home. She is no longer able to participate in that program. We would tweak or adjust our care circle as needed to make sure that our support was as evenly distributed among us as possible and that everyone is able to take care of themselves and enjoy our own lives and families. It is a difficult and delicate organization to maintain.

Our system does not always work perfectly but we are generally very satisfied and grateful for what we have been able to provide for our mom. We all share the view that mom is our priority and that her comfort, happiness, and peace are paramount. COVID has presented an added layer of stress and challenge. It has impacted each of us in so many ways. And it has stretched our ability to do as we once did with relative ease. I mentioned mom's own decline. Added to that is the reality that we are

not spring chickens ourselves, now in our 60's and 70s. Some of us are still working or facing the issues as our peers, issues such as financial stability, how and where we will age, supporting our own children and grandchildren, and our desire to continue to enjoy our own lives. Because of COVID, we are no longer able to call in additional support from the outside of our family pod, so it is really the seven of us.

Let me add that each of us brings something special and sweet to mom. Our time and interaction with her are precious and allow us to be a part of her life in ways that we may not have in the past. We bring to our new relationship with her, at this stage, our own unique personalities, and ways of engaging with her. These days she is never alone. We make sure that her medical needs are attended to and that her life remains rich with family memories and stories, laughter and joking, the foods that she enjoys, her favorite TV shows, occasional rides to visit our father's grave, or time shared just sitting on the porch and greeting neighbors. She looks forward to her Sunday morning church attendance by Zoom and gospel music in the mornings. Her day is not complete without speaking to and hearing of and from her two youngest children and their families in Miami. It helps very much that she is a very pleasant person most times and very cooperative. She has been teaching us lessons in aging, lessons in acceptance, lessons in continuing to fight for our dignified aging. People marvel at what we have built to support her and one another. To us, it is a given.

On the morning of the scariest day of my time with mom, I rode in the front of the ambulance as my sister followed in her car, Although

frightened, I felt a sense of calm and peace. While we say often and sometimes in jest, that mom may outlive all of us, we are acutely aware that she is 98 years old. Thankfully, she has avoided serious falls, COVID, and other serious illnesses. She is only on one medication and maybe another one or two as needed. Like many of her generation, her faith and belief in God is very strong as is her readiness to go from this Earth when her time comes.

What I hope doesn't crack is her (and our!) belief that we have given her the best of what we can give, that we held back nothing, that we worked together to make sure that she receives the love and care that she always showed us and taught us. We may falter or fall short sometimes but what I know for sure is that each of us in our own ways and then us collectively honor her each day with our demonstrations of love and sacrifice. We have a system and an organization for her support that seems seamless and well-oiled. But we are humans with our own needs and desires. What we know for sure is that she gave us a gift of love for her and one another. I can't imagine even a small crack in that generous and valuable lesson of family love and respect for our mom who gave (and continues) to give us much to follow and to incorporate into our own lives. *Thank you, Mom, our Queen, our Matriarch, for your example, your sacrifices, and all that you continue to give to us and the generations that follow.*

Reflections

_____
_____
_____
_____
_____
_____
_____
_____
_____
_____
_____
_____
_____
_____
_____
_____
_____
_____

Breathe
Monique S. Johnson

The day I found a revelatory note card on my daughter's nightstand answered questions that had periodically tiptoed across my mind over the years. The card had one word prominently written across its blank canvas—ensuring that it would receive undivided attention from any gaze. It read, BREATHE. At that moment I felt an immediate sense of calm as I unconsciously heeded the prompt. At the same time, anxiety bubbled up as I thought about the circumstances that could have prompted her to create this visible reminder.

> *"There are years that ask questions and there are years that answer."*
> *Zora Neale Hurston*

The BREATHE note card marked a difficult year of transition for my daughter. It was her first year of high school and full of foreign, uncomfortable and overwhelming experiences. She had been in a supportive and nurturing Montessori environment during her formative years. These environments encouraged independence and collaboration; they encouraged social awareness and empathy. Montessori honors the unique developmental needs of every child and tailors learning to meet those needs. To develop her leadership and reinforce learning, she was encouraged to mentor and teach younger students. This community

allowed her to discover and appreciate who she was and to imagine the possibilities of what could be.

Her high school is an academically rigorous environment where all of the students are high achieving, driven and future focused. The size of her freshman class was about the size of the entire K-8 Montessori program. The norms associated with high school were all foreign to her. Different teachers for each class, longer class times, homework, and regular test taking, various extracurricular activities and sports, navigating class changes and locker room changing, eating in the cafeteria, trying to find a tribe, and figuring out where you fit in. And most of all, for her it signified a loss of community. I had forgotten how difficult high school can be until I watched her struggle almost every morning to muster the courage and energy to get out of bed. I saw mild signs of anxiety beginning to creep in and finding the note card immediately made me realize how tangible and taxing her struggle was. It also opened a floodgate of memories from my experiences at exactly her age. However, in addition to those same high school experiences, at age 15 I was also supporting my mother in her struggle with schizoaffective disorder.

We must accept the end of something in order to begin to build something new.

My mother's first manic episode occurred when I was nine. My recall of that period is hazy, but the roller coaster ride of her mental health breakdowns is vivid. At that time, no one understood what triggered her breakdown or the severity of her disorder. She was able to

function for several months at a time with no erratic or concerning behavior. However, over the years I learned that during those seemingly calm periods, she struggled to maintain her peace. Life struggles would send her on a downward spiral. She hallucinated causing her to believe that those who loved her the most were conspiring against her. She would turn angry and violent and then break down into unshakable depression. I could not leave the house because she feared for my safety. After I snuck out many times to attend school, she would arrive there irate. The administrators knew something was wrong and tried to shield me from her irrational demands.

My family was supportive but grew weary of the constant shifts and imbalances. They had their own immediate struggles with poverty and underemployment, which are all too common among families in the Black community. Like many Black families, they saw mental illness as a sign of weakness and a ploy for attention. They thought that my mother could be stirred back into a lucid state like shaking someone awake from a nightmare. I knew that was not possible after witnessing her fight to stay on the functional side of sanity. She tried to care for me and my needs, going to work when she could, taking me to school, leaving me notes to remind me to do my homework or begin dinner. She wanted so much to stay well and to be happy, but that aspiration seemed to constantly allude her.

The year I turned 15 marked the year when I began to take on more responsibility for helping my mother manage her mental health. I developed a sixth sense and could tell when there were changes in her

behavior that could lead to manic episodes and hospitalizations. While eager to drive, craving the freedom like any teenager, I also recognized that this ability enabled me to better serve as her advocate and caretaker. Navigating the normal vicissitudes of high school—academic expectations, friends, playing sports and taunting boys—was an escape and refuge from the uncertainty that blanketed my home. Although the source of my daughter's stress was different from mine at her age, after reading that note card, I deeply understood why she had to remind herself to breathe.

Women and girls of color, in particular, face unique stressors that are compounded by the intersection of race and gender identities. Negative sociocultural experiences rooted in racism, discrimination, and sexism contribute to emotional pain, but often remain unacknowledged as sources of distress[19]. Children of color experience substantially higher rates of adversity during childhood than their white peers, which can significantly impact physical and mental health, as well as educational and economic outcomes. African American females, grades 9-12, were 70 percent[20] more likely to attempt suicide in 2017, as compared to non-Hispanic white females of the same age. However, a study showed

---

[19] https://www.law.georgetown.edu/poverty-inequality-center/wp-content/uploads/sites/14/2019/12/Mental-Health-and-Girls-of-Color.pdf

[20] https://minorityhealth.hhs.gov/omh/browse.aspx?lvl=4&lvlid=24

that 63%[21] of African Americans believe that a mental health condition is a personal sign of weakness. This belief system subconsciously permeates our culture, making it difficult for Black women who struggle under the weight of mental health conditions to seek support.

The decade after high school enabled me to escape and comfortably focus on discovering who I was and who I wanted to be. Then a manic explosion occurred, leaving my stepfather—who had stepped into my shoes—at a loss. He soldiered through the patterns of ups and downs, but the last violent exchange was too much for him to handle. He sent my mother to live with me. I was 28. Leaning on my sister circle of mental health therapists and social workers was my saving grace. Going back and forth to doctors in her hometown to learn more about her history and diagnosis while trying to find the right mental health professionals in my community became the norm. The blessings of healthcare coverage became immediately evident because the medication, therapy, and hospitalizations would have bankrupted me. In that first year my mother spent about four months in area hospitals. Doctors experimented with medications, but nothing seemed to help her stabilize so hospitalizations became the norm.

I vividly recall a conversation with a psychologist while getting my mother connected with services in my community. The doctor asked,

---

[21] Ward EC, Wiltshire JC, Detry MA, Brown RL. "African American men and women's attitude toward mental illness, perceptions of stigma, and preferred coping behaviors". Nurs Res. 2013 May-Jun;62(3):185-94. doi: 10.1097/NNR.0b013e31827bf533. PMID: 23328705; PMCID: PMC4279858.

"How are you doing?" I did not quite understand the underlying interest but appreciated her concern. I responded that I was exhausted but handling the demands okay. To that she said, "If you have not exhibited any symptoms of mental illness, then you should be okay. You've passed the age where those symptoms usually appear." Nevertheless, she encouraged me to stay aware for the benefit of my future offspring due to the genetic characteristics of psychiatric disorders. "Would the genetics of mental illness manifest in my child?" That was one of the questions I asked fifteen years ago after the birth of my daughter. That note card served as a reminder but also an indicator of how knowledge and vigilant awareness can help us encourage mentally healthy habits in our children.

Over the years, my mother has stabilized, and she is able to function independently with wraparound support. Working to model self-care practices, encouraging my daughter to embrace her feelings, and allowing her to witness my journey are my priorities. By modeling these practices for my daughter, I hope to remove the stigma of mental health disorders and normalize mental health self-care. These principles have been critical along my journey.

This journey with my mother is instrumental in helping me to cultivate curious awareness. A primary reason why the stigma of mental illnesses exists is because their origins are difficult to pinpoint and the manifestations vary. Physical illnesses are more comforting because we can usually see how and where the trauma impacts the individuals, and the symptoms align with scientific study. There is so much yet to be

discovered and uncovered about the brain and its complex functionality. Nevertheless, awareness is a source of empowerment. Scientific understanding is critical to dispelling myths and overcoming stigma. Having that understanding serves as a source of grounding on which to build.

As a caregiver, I have learned that modeling self-care is critical to my physical and emotional health. The self-care movement has made us much more aware of our well-being. However, it has also led us to believe that there are specific practices that should be ascribed to, but this could not be further from the truth. Self-care can include anything from drinking your morning coffee from your favorite coffee cup to a regular yoga practice. It can include morning meditation or taking a deep breath before engaging in a conversation. The practices are our own to identify, develop, and manage. The only requirement from my perspective is non-judgement. We should be open to trying new approaches but not feel beholden to any of them. They can change with each passing day or become traditions and rituals that we maintain for years to come. Yoga, meditation, and journaling are three of my self-care practices, but I have many. I try on new ones and discard those that do not authentically serve me.

On a regular basis I attempt to create connection through active listening while engaging with my mother and daughter. Active listening is a way of listening and responding that improves mutual understanding. The verbal and non-verbal cues indicate present moment engagement within these conversations. Some of those non-verbal cues

include eye contact, leaning forward or nodding, allowing someone to finish what he or she is saying without interruption, and giving them time to respond. Verbal cues include restating, reflecting and asking open-ended questions with interest and without being intrusive. Using this approach usually creates comfort and a space for connection by unlocking new ways of seeing and thinking. Within the context of my conversations with my daughter, I find that active listening empowers her to process her thoughts verbally in a judgement free zone. Having these safe spaces are critical to mental and emotional well-being.

Along this caregiving journey I have discovered the importance of showing vulnerability and sharing my stories. Being vulnerable can be terrifying. The notion that revealing my inner most thoughts, feelings, and fears will be judged or used as a means to expose me can be debilitating. In part that is because weaknesses are viewed as shortcomings thereby giving them and others the power to harm us. When I reframe vulnerability as a source of power and an authentic expression of my journey, I may feel the fear, but I do it anyway. In this space, I tend to push against the victimization of shame and inadequacy. We recognize the resiliency that resides in the suffering. Sharing my journey and my stories with my daughter has been cathartic and it also removes the stigma. She sees me coordinating medication, collaborating with doctors, monitoring, caretaking. She sees my weariness and my tears one day and my focused energy the next. I do not hide the yin and the yang because both are necessary on this journey. Because I do not hide, I believe that she has developed more

compassion and empathy for my mom, for me, and most importantly, for herself.

The questions that I constantly asked over the years, narrated my search for meaning. "Why me? What will this mean for my child? What has the experience come to teach me? How will this experience help me to fulfill my divine assignment?" There had to be a purpose in the pain and my spiritual grounding will not allow me to believe otherwise. A learning from my mother's journey was that part of my purpose rested in being an advocate, witness, and supporter for others. I also discovered through the BREATHE note card that my learning on that journey was leaving a legacy of mental wellness, discovery, and courage for future generations.

Reflections

Once A Woman...Twice A Child
Alice A. Brown

Our precious 98-year-old Mother, our "Queen," is aging in place while
experiencing various life stages,
Though her endless tomorrows are now limited, cherished memories
now long forgotten, we constantly sing her praises!

She is a timeless, vintage, lovable woman who struggles to piece her
past and thoughts together,
She relies on our coaching to help stimulate her mind and expressions,
then her face brightens, and her smile appears to last forever.

Mom taught us how to walk and talk, dress, pray and to entrust her "old
school" rearing,
How to share our food, our time, our thoughts, love and to be humble
and endearing.

Now we assist her with walking, communicating, meal planning, attire,
hygiene and we try to minimize her challenges and fears,
We exercise a tremendous amount of patience with kindness like she
demonstrated over the years.

She treated our illnesses with old home remedies or arranged for
doctors' house calls,
We now arrange for in-home doctors to provide physicals,
prescriptions, and all.
Mom's melodic voice fills the air with religious songs and humming
praises with deep devotion,
She reminds us of the hummingbirds that frequent her flowers with
their magical wings in motion.
She is our dedicated advocate who always made sacrifices regardless of
our situation or condition.
We are now her devoted advocate for health, wellness, regardless of her
situation and declined cognition.

As kids, she checked on us throughout the night to ensure our security,
warmth and peace,
We now monitor her throughout the night to ensure comfort, normal
chest compressions while she is asleep.

On a 24/7 rotational basis we care for Mom diligently and honorably
oftentimes with little rest,
Our well-orchestrated caregiving may generate moments of anxieties
and stress.

The painful memories of losing her elder son and husband we believe
still resides in her heart and mind,
Now her mortality dominates our thoughts with sorrow and fright—she
has fewer loving years ahead and more blessed ones behind.

Mom used to quote from her Bible, "Once a Man, Twice a Child," which
we didn't understand for a long while,
She and we are all actively engaged in her precious world, "Once a
"Woman," Twice a Child."

We honor Mrs. Mabra Iola Brown—Our Mother, Our Queen!

It is speculated that the positive perceptions associated with caregiving, combined with one's own resourcefulness may buffer against the impact of negative emotional distress, such as anxiety, depression, and hostility for African American caregivers.

Socioeconomic and demographic factors modify observed relationship between caregiving intensity and three dimensions of quality of life in informal adult children caregivers, Cook et al Health and Quality of Life Outcomes, 2018

Reflections

Caregiver to the End
Pamela Ferrell Neal

I moved from Rhode Island to Washington, DC to go to college. At that time, I met my future husband and in-laws. Mama and Papa were like my second set of parents. As they got older, my husband and I became their caregivers. They lived independently in their own home. By the time they turned 80, we convinced them to stop driving (for safety reasons) and were responsible for taking them to doctor appointments, plant stores, dinner outings, and wherever they needed to go. My husband made daily visits to their home to mow the lawn and prepare their meals. Fortunately, we owned our business and lived 10 minutes away so that we could do this. They were 80 years old when our children were born, so it was super special to watch them enjoy grandparenting and interacting with babies at their age.

At age 86, Papa passed before his wife, so I established a routine of calling Mama in the morning before arriving with breakfast. This particular morning, she did not answer; it was unusual for her not to pick up the phone because she loved the telephone. It was her lifeline to friends and family. After calling several times with no answer, my six-year-old son and I went to the house and found her lying on the floor. She was conscious but appeared to have fractured her hip during a nighttime fall. The thought of her on the floor alone for hours was disheartening and all the more reason I believed she should move in with us. She

enjoyed her own home. If only she wore the Life Alert necklace. What's the point of having it if you don't wear it?

The ambulance driver hesitantly took her to the hospital of her choice—he said the ER was slow and would keep us waiting. We did wait, but I came prepared with snacks and mama's bag of vitamins and medication she took daily, including the baby aspirin she faithfully took every morning. I wanted the doctors to know what medications she was taking.

She was admitted and called me the following day to say, "Bring me some bottled water because the hospital water tastes terrible." When my husband, the children, and I arrived at the hospital, she was not in her room. I asked the nurse at the desk where she was, and to my surprise, she was in the ICU. I had spoken to Mama two hours ago. In the ICU room, she was in a coma, and a nurse was seated at a table staring at the beeping machine hooked to her. Still, no answers for what happened. I was very forceful to get a detail report of everything that transpired since I hung up the phone with her that morning.

I was angry, sad, and shocked that the doctor gave her a blood thinner when she was already taking the baby aspirin every day. The combination of the aspirin and blood thinner caused her blood to thin too much and it caused bleeding on the brain. She would die three days later. Mama did not die from old age, she died because medical professionals did not take the time to evaluate her medications. Who knows how much longer Mama would have been able to enjoy her grandchildren or have engaging telephone conversations with family and friends had those

entrusted with her medical care done what was expected of them. We were robbed of those days, weeks, months, or years. This experience has led me to profoundly understand the need for medical advocates to help our loved ones demand the care and attention they so rightly deserve.

Reflections

Honour Thy Father and Mother
Dorothy J. James

My mother, Lena James was born April 16, 1920. She transitioned on May 13, 2014, at the age of 94 and only a few weeks after her birthday. For approximately five years, I had the privilege and honor to be a primary caregiver for my mother. At the time of such occurrence, we lived in our family home on Palm Avenue in Lynwood, California. Lynwood is a small suburban city in Los Angeles County. After my father transitioned, I moved in with my mother to help her acclimate to her new life as a widow. At the ripe age of 73, she had never lived alone (literally) nor on her own, as she was married from her family's home in 1938 directly to a home that she and my father shared as husband and wife. I am one of ten daughters that my parents raised in the City of Los Angeles.

My mother was an excellent housekeeper, a profound tailor, a devoted wife, mother, and grandmother. She was also the mother of her church, All Saints Church of God In Christ which is in Downey, California. Going to Sunday church services, Bible Study and prayer meetings was among some of her most favorite life activities. She also loved to garden and cook especially for the holiday season. In her last days, she was unable to do any of these things and her decline was obvious.

My mother was a very busy and active woman during the years of my father's life. She was a very important and nurturing force in our

family and was very happy and secure in herself. There were certain responsibilities that she didn't have to worry about while my father was alive; however, upon his passing, I saw that she had become very anxious about those areas of her life. She became very quiet and sometimes anxious about life and life circumstances. I remember him saying to her as he was passing under hospice care, "You're going to have to take care of yourself now" in a very warm and caring way, and she started crying. My mother and father spent all their time together as they were married for 54 years prior to his death.

My caregiving was not planned and was the result of my father's passing. I became a caregiver to my mother while she was still somewhat physically healthy but challenged in other significant ways. She and I both agreed that it would be good for us to live together since she needed financial help and assistance. At the time, I was divorced with one child, a teenage son, who also moved in with us and was somewhat unhappy about my decision. However, living with and helping my mother had its mutual benefits since having someone at home with my son while I worked long hours was an ideal situation. My mother's three-bedroom home was spacious and provided adequate space for the three of us. The romper room and swimming pool were instrumental in placating my reluctant son. Shortly after I moved in, she began to slow down a bit and I learned that her blood pressure medication was increased by her doctor shortly after the passing of my father.

After my father's death, my mother became more withdrawn, almost to a point of being secretly anxious about financial matters. I lived

with my mom and cared for her while she was still physically well with very few health limitations, however, she was not completely capable of taking care of her own personal needs and financial business affairs such as banking, transportation, accounting, and paying bills. And other life decisions, in a way, were unfamiliar to her. Sometimes she worried needlessly about finances, although time and time again I assured her that I could take care of her small and minimum financial needs.

During the five years of living with and caring for my mom, my siblings seldom came by or called. They did not help me with ANYTHING! Further, they hardly visited except occasionally and on a few holidays during the year. I don't really know why they were somewhat distant. I would like to believe that it was because they knew that I was there with her and that I would take excellent care of her and her needs. Many times, I wanted to confront them about their behavior, but my mother didn't want me to say a word to them about their behavior. I learned that she avoided confrontation at all costs. She could not express, exert control, or show her emotions at all. It appeared that she kept her pain and suffering to herself.

After being a caregiver for my mother for five years, from 1994 through December 1, 1999, I moved and one of my other siblings with 5 children moved in with my mother due to an urgent necessity.

Just two weeks prior to my mother's passing, I lost one of my sisters to breast cancer. It appeared that her passing triggered my mother's downward spiral and eventual passing. Needless to say, we had their funerals within two weeks of each other. My recently departed

sister had spent a few months earlier providing caregiving to my mom before her own passing. The two of them spent a lot of quality hours together before both of their deaths.

Some of the most beautiful moments we shared were our Sunday time together at church and our planned Sunday dinners. Mom was the "Mother" of the church, and I was the church musician. We spent hours together at home chit chatting about the events and affairs of the church. My mother was a praying woman, a very spiritual woman. I will always remember how she dedicated herself to God and proclaimed her relationship with God as that of a wife and husband.

My advice to anyone who is going through the experience of caregiving for a parent or parents is to love them unconditionally. Hang in there regardless of how difficult and impossible they may make the tasks because of stubbornness or unwillingness to cooperate at times. Love and honor them for who they truly are, i.e., your parent(s) because you never know how much more time you may have left with them. Treasure them in so many ways and remember their wise sayings and their wise ways.

Overall, and through it all, I wouldn't trade anything for the experience, journey, and time in which I companioned my mom during this lifetime. I count it as a tremendous blessing having the opportunity to live with my mother for five years after my father's transition and to grow closer to her and the opportunity to know her in a very intimate way. It was one of my life's most blessed experiences.

When family caregivers do not have training, support, and opportunities for rest and self-care, their own health, well-being, and quality of life suffer.

2022 National Strategy to Support Family Caregivers, RAISE Act Family Caregivers Advisory Council and the Advisory Council to Support Grandparents Raising Grandchildren, 2022

Reflections

Caregiver for Momma
Rayetta Wheeler-Rice

Caregiving my aging mother (Jean) brought with it responsibilities that no one could get me ready for. I watched my best friend and hero slowly become weak and frail day after day after day. This broke my heart seeing her this way, making this the hardest task I had to do. In my story, I will share how much I wanted to show my mother love and not force control over her while being her caregiver.

Jean was born on July 11, 1934, and she married Charles (Ray) Wheeler and had six children. She was a beloved mother and an amazing nana to her grandchildren and great grandchildren, and she was a faithful servant to her Lord. She was a longtime resident of Maywood Illinois. Graduating from her local high school Proviso East, she advanced her education and graduated from Moody Bible Institute in Chicago, Illinois. She worked at Alden's in Chicago Illinois, and later become a secretary at AG Communication Systems in Northlake, Illinois, where she retired.

Jean was a community action type person working with the Girl Scouts at the local grade school in Maywood Illinois. Christmas was her favorite time of year—she always made homemade stockings for everyone she knew. Everything Jean did was life and love affirming with her strength and power. She was known for her big wide smile and patience.

My mother, or "Momma," as I called her, was diagnosed with heart disease and high blood pressure with early signs of dementia. So, in 2014, I started working with the Community Care facility helping her out two days a week with shopping, cleaning, and washing her clothes. I joined her care team at Loyola Hospital taking her to the doctor and administering medications—the two days a week became four hours every day. I wanted so much for her to regain her independence and enjoy life as she used to. In the days ahead she continued going to church, sewing with her senior friends, and assisting at the senior site serving lunch.

In 2017, she suffered a stroke, which **was the scariest day of my life.** Knowing this, mother tried to take care of herself to keep her independence but couldn't, so my days increased to seven days a week. **After the stroke, her disease progressed making every step a battle.** In my mind I was thinking, how hard can this be? I mean, we are talking about a woman who in the past knew all of her six children's birthdays, social security numbers, as well as those for her ten grandchildren. Well, only God knew the battles we had in front of us with swelling in her legs, trying different medications for her blood pressure, ulcers, wound care, and ICU, managing doctors' appointments, and handling her bills. Finally, the role changed to me becoming the parent and she the daughter. **Mother made it clear to the family that** *the nursing home, was out of the question.* **She wanted to be at home and, giving thanks to God, we were able to grant her wish.** Never did I imagine that taking care of a parent would be so challenging. But I was still up for the challenge, thinking she would get

better, and when it didn't happen, her doctors had to come up with another plan.

As time went on, I found my emotions kicking in—going from fear to anger within minutes. Then here comes another emotion to deal with: guilt. Why guilt? I never thought about her emotions, how scared she must be hearing her diagnosis and what to do about her future.

Whenever she was not herself, she would say, "You are going to miss me when I'm gone." And she was right. Every minute of the day I really miss her and the sound of her voice. I learned a lot from my mother. We became even closer than before. *One lesson was patience and more patience because now* <u>dementia was taking her mind</u>. On her better days, my mother knew who I was, where she lived and what day it was. So, when she didn't, I said to myself, "Oh my. Houston, we have a problem." She went from being brilliant, cognizant, and independent enough to take care her personal needs to a person so weak in pain that she couldn't sit up for long periods of time which caused her trouble relaxing at night. Those days were the hardest because she didn't know what or why her body hurt so much, and I didn't have the answer.

I would hear someone crying and, guess what? It was me crying. The medication wasn't helping, and her dementia was making it hard for her to follow commands. I felt like I failed her. I needed God's help to forgive me for not being able to care for my mother. Every morning was a struggle in the weeks to come. I would walk into another room and cry. One day I took a breath and said, "Please, God. Help me remember I am

doing my best and give me wisdom." God answered me saying, "You can't do this by yourself," so I got others involved.

In 2020, two weeks before Christmas, Momma was not responding to me calling her name. The paramedic told us she was stable, but I felt something was different. This made me worry more. Because of the Covid epidemic, I couldn't be with her and could only exchange phone calls back and forth with my sister, brother, and doctors. According to Medicare policy, I could not serve as Momma's caregiver and power of attorney during this period, so my sister took on the role of power of attorney. During her final days, she drifted in and out of consciousness, and her body began to reject all treatment. To cope, I turned to God with prayer to watch over my Momma. I prayed to God to not take my mother from me. I could not imagine my life without her. I finally realized my prayer was selfish. I was only thinking about myself and not her. I asked God to keep my mother safe, grant her peace, and He did answer my prayer: my mother died on Christmas Eve morning.

In life she was a special person who touched everyone's life and who was cherished in the hearts of her friends and family. She leaves a legacy behind—always spending her time volunteering and lending a helping hand whenever she was needed. She also loved to impart important life lessons to everyone. She loved the Lord and always reminded her family and friends of how "good God is" and "to keep Him first with wherever you do." Her favorite Christian song was "I Am Redeemed." She was most proud of her accomplishments with her children, grandchildren, and great grandchildren, and working with the

Homebound Ministry, Superintendent at Rock of Ages Baptist Church in Maywood, Illinois, under the pastorage of Reverend Marvin E. Wiley, Operation Uplift in Maywood, Illinois and helping with the seniors. In her pastime, she would crochet and knit with her friends at the community center.

I want to end my story by saying, caregiver, you can't do it alone! When change becomes overwhelming, ask for help. Caregiving has many responsibilities and many rewards, and I would also like to thank you caregivers all you do, and may God continue to grant you strength, courage, and patience.

Reflections

_____

_____

_____

_____

_____

_____

_____

_____

_____

_____

_____

_____

_____

_____

_____

_____

_____

_____

_____

_____

_____

My Mother Doesn't Know Me
Ivy A. Lewis

I am the middle child. I have a sister almost two years older and a brother ten years younger. I'm 62 years old and have been my mother's caregiver since 2013, although she has resided in an assisted living home with up to 6 other seniors since 2018. I left home and New York City in January 1979 to complete my undergraduate studies in Delaware and two years later moved to Illinois for graduate school. I didn't live with my mother again until I moved her in with me in 1999 after purchasing a home in Maryland. We decided it made sense for us to live together since we were both unmarried—it also freed me from multiple monthly trips to Chesapeake, Virginia (where she relocated after retiring), to check on her.

Our house grew to five occupants in 2002, and I became a member of the "sandwich generation"[22]—living with my mother and her eldest sister <u>and</u> two teenagers after their mother, my cousin and my aunt's daughter, passed away. Fast forward to 2009 and again it was just mother and me. In 2010 we agreed to move her into a senior apartment building to avoid the loneliness she experienced while I spent hours at work. After a year's worth of complaining about this, that, and the other

---

[22] A generation of people, typically in their 30s or 40s, responsible for raising their own children and caring for aging parents.

thing, my siblings and I agreed that mother might be happier living closer to the grands—my brother's children, in upstate New York. In 2013, we knew something was wrong. She adamantly and regularly accused my brother of entering her apartment at night eating her cookies, drinking her sodas, and moving or taking other stuff she couldn't find. She also forgot visits and calls from my sister and me. When I visited, I'd see multiples of the same food items in her refrigerator—eggs, bacon, butter, cheese, etc. She'd put these same items on her grocery list week after week for my sister-in-law to pick up for her. I observed that she didn't recognize these items when she looked into the refrigerator and would think she'd run out of them. A trip to the doctor's office identified the problem—Alzheimer's dementia. So began my caregiver journey.

I moved mother back in with me and for the next five years I saw her memory worsen and physical conditions decline while my love for her grew. Mother used a three-wheeled walker for years (she called it her "mobilette"), as years of sciatic pain caused her to stoop over permanently and to need its support. The progressive memory loss and physical decline made her so vulnerable to me. In turn it made me her fierce protector. At the same time, she was a handful. To get her to bathe was a ritual of pleadings, tears (hers or mine or hers <u>and</u> mine), threats to withhold the morning coffee, name calling—I was the meanest person she knew—and, finally, acquiescence, on her part or mine. I didn't always win. When I did, it wasn't with her full capitulation. I had to cajole her every step of the way. But the process was not without humor. Getting her to remove her partial dentures was like pulling teeth, causing another

round of name calling. Yet I was never satisfied that she brushed her remaining teeth sufficiently. So, I brushed them like you would a two-year-old, which always made her chuckle. I brushed like she had a mouth full of teeth. While she could wash her face, I would always clean out her nostrils like I'd seen her do many times. That always made her laugh. I was going for the gold. Then I'd have to cajole or threaten to walk out, or both, to get her into the tub for a shower. She'd sit on a shower chair until it was time to wash her private parts. For the life of me I could not wash my mother's vagina—I may need a therapist to understand why. Instead, I'd wash everything else and ask her to wash her "particulars," a word she would repeat with humor. I would threaten to do so until the washcloth came out clean which would either provoke a laugh from her or scorn.

Afterwards, dressing her from top to bottom always evoked tenderness from one of us. She would abruptly kiss my arm, face, shoulder, or whatever part of me was nearest to her lips when she got the notion. It was an expression of thanks for my determination (as I forged ahead despite her protestations) and level of care. At times she would actually thank me out loud for taking such good care of her. How my heart would swell with love for her at these moments. While the dementia showed up regularly, she'd be on point, in the moment, just as much. So, I knew she understood her circumstances and the scope of her care. Her vulnerability and my ability to care for and protect her made me so emotional at times. It felt right to play this role in my mother's life even with the daily challenges and stresses I faced.

On one of the numerous occasions, I sought refuge in my sister's ear to meet the challenges of the day, my cousin, who was riding shotgun with me in my car with sister on the speaker phone, reminded me of my mother's love of gospel music (Mother sang in church choirs for years). Cousin, with my sister "amen"-ing in the background, suggested I use it to set the mood each day. My brother had already given me the tools— Mahalia Jackson CDs that mother loved most among her gospel collection. What a difference that made in getting our day started in a good place, including through the shower ritual as I would play it loud enough for a sing-along in the bathroom.

I would test my mother's memory from time to time and on one occasion received an unexpected response. At this point, it was clear her short-term memory had steadily declined. She would forget that she'd eaten dinner, been to the senior daycare center on a given day, went to the bathroom multiple times in an hour, just had a glass of water. One day, while visiting my brother and his family, I asked her to name her children because by this time she didn't use my name very much. She named all three of us - Ivy, Cynthia, and Mark. I was encouraged until I asked her, "Who am I?"

She said she didn't know.

I said, "I'm your daughter."

She harrumphed in disbelief and disagreement. When I persisted, she said, "Why didn't anyone tell me I had another daughter?" I blurted out, "Mother doesn't know I'm her daughter"

She repeated, "Why didn't anyone tell me ...?"

The look on my 13-year-old niece's face was priceless—she later asked her mother if she would forget her, too, which concerned her because she "planned to get her pension."

I saw over time that while my mother refused to believe that I was Ivy, she never complained that I didn't call or visit her, a regular complaint she lodged at my sister and brother. I believe subconsciously she knows I—Ivy— am with her, or that I have become an acceptable substitute. To this day, when I visit mother in the assisted living home and someone says, "Ivy is here," looking directly in my face she asks, "Where is she?"

While I was away at Exhale, an annual retreat of 40+ beautiful Black women, and mother in the care of my sister and cousin, my mother stopped walking. After 30 hours in the ER and two days in the hospital, she was going to be released. I returned on the day the hospital planned to release her though she still could not walk. According to the medical professionals—doctors, social worker, head nurse—not walking is not a medical issue. Realization hit hard! If mother couldn't walk, I couldn't take care of her in our home any longer.

Mother's first assisted living home didn't work out. She was understandably confused about why she had to stay there and without me. While she didn't know me as her daughter, she knew me as her caregiver. I belonged. And honestly, she didn't like the owner/caregiver. Mother quickly proved to be too much for the women to handle. The caregiver and I reached the same conclusion after just two weeks. Mother had to go! She'd likely be dead by now if she hadn't left that home. There

were signs of neglect. During week two, I discovered a blister on my mother's heel half the size of a golf ball that was not being treated (it took weeks of intense wound care to heal it) and a urinary tract infection being treated with cranberry supplements.

In less than 30 days mother was in her second assisted living residence where she lives to this day. With God's help I found a home with loving and competent care, just minutes from the first.

Mother is still a handful. She still fights the daily bath, more intensely now that someone else is washing her "particulars"; is embarrassed that she soils herself; believes she can and does walk; and continues (even after three years) to ask me if I've come to take her home. In her heart, and mind, she belongs with me because I am her caregiver, whether she recognizes Ivy or not. I don't expect that to change because I am and continue to be her caretaker.

Minority residents tend to be disproportionately served in "lower-tier" urban facilities characterized by poor resources (such as heavy reliance on Medicaid reimbursement), lower staffing level and higher staff turnover rate, and inferior quality of care. These inferior facility characteristics seem to be driving part of the disparities in social engagement as suggested by our sequential analyses.

Yue Li, PhD and Xueya Cai, PhD. Racial and Ethnic Disparities in Social Engagement Among US Nursing Home Residents, 2014.

Reflections

_____
_____
_____
_____
_____
_____
_____
_____
_____
_____
_____
_____
_____
_____
_____
_____
_____
_____
_____
_____
_____
_____

FOR THEM I WEEP: A Letter to Mama
Dyone Massey-Mitchell

I sat by your bed today, Mama, I gently combed your hair
and although you never spoke a word, I know you felt me there
I held your hand today, Mama, until you fell asleep
and as I thought of happier times, I slowly started to weep
Tears filled my eyes and ran down my face until I could barely see
but then I began to realize that these tears were not for me

You have great-grandchildren now, Mama
who were robbed, even though they don't know it,
of the Southern comfort from a strong black woman
who now can no longer show it

We have new neighbors now, Mama, your vibrance they'll never know
The feisty woman who took no crap but made friends wherever she'd go
They won't taste your cakes, your homemade pies
or tasty treats straight from your oven...
Your down home cooking and homemade bread
made from scratch and plenty of lovin'

The choir you loved to sing with...you were so happy then...
and although your friends still ask about you, they won't hear you sing again
For the Christmases at home that you cannot share
for the children playing everywhere
for the one-on-one company we use to keep
it is for these things that I weep

To the nurses who care for you...the doctors who are there for you
To them I wanna scream out loud...this shell of a woman is not who she is
because my mama is graceful and proud!

I weep for the senseless unkind things that cause our family drama
but I weep not for the regal queen
who was...and still is...my Mama

Written for my mother-in-law, Ms. Eula Mae Beach, on behalf of her daughter
Ms. Bonita Mitchell Robinson.

"[M]y thought is that in a minority community that has faced severe hardship and discrimination, an ethic of internal mutual reliance long ago became part of its culture as a survival strategy. Feeling connected to and responsible for one another gives each individual a greater chance to succeed. When faced with a caregiving challenge now, that same network of support kicks in naturally."

Barry J. Jacobs, AARP. Community and Culture Help Black Caregivers Cope With the Challenges of Family Caregiving. 2021
https://www.aarp.org/caregiving/basics/info-2021/african-american-caregivers-cope-better.html

Reflections

_____
_____
_____
_____
_____
_____
_____
_____
_____
_____
_____
_____
_____
_____
_____
_____
_____
_____
_____
_____
_____

Caregiver Chronicles: From Discovery to Decline
Sound Whisdom

THE MOM EDITION

Was it the heart murmur from birth, Willie Mae?

Was it the stress of each day, Willie Mae?

Was it you being the oldest with all brothers, Willie Mae?

Was it the move from Alabama to Illinois, Willie Mae?

Was it the Spiegel Outlet way Willie Mae?

Did South Chicago Community Hospital treat you right, Willie Mae?

Did my brother Robert's father make you fight, Willie Mae?

Did Edward Allen make it right, Willie Mae?

Did my brother Ed and I enrich your life, Willie Mae?

Did my father's gambling create strife, Willie Mae?

Then, why did your heart have to be so weak?

Then, why did the pacemaker not keep beat?

Then, why did my life include so much unknown?

Then, why did I have to take care of you on my own?

Then, why is this mom edition—a part of my mental condition?

THE DAD EDITION

Was it the veil when you were born, Mr. MoJo?

Was it the Georgia life of scorn, Mr. MoJo?

Was it the orange picking from Florida, Mr. MoJo?

Was it the Korean War trauma, Mr. MoJo?

Was it the Policy wars, Mr. MoJo?

Did ballroom dancing fulfill your life, Mr. MoJo?

Did you have the greatest wife, Mr. MoJo?

Did you almost lose your life, Mr. MoJo?

Did you make 1972 Black Mailman of the Year, Mr. MoJo?

Did you spread lots of cheer in Illinois, Mr. MoJo?

Then, why did your brain change up the game?

Then, why did you forget even my name?

Then, why did your body forget how to eat?

Then, why was the only consistent caregiver me?

Then, why is this dad edition—stained in my intuition?

Reflections

_____
_____
_____
_____
_____
_____
_____
_____
_____
_____
_____
_____
_____
_____
_____
_____
_____
_____
_____

10 Things We Learned

1. Hospice care is not only for end-of-life care. I discovered that Original Medicare does not cover hospice care services, the patient must be moved to Medicare Hospice. A patient can be transferred back to Original Medicare after selecting Medicare Hospice, if warranted.

2. I learned that Urinary Tract Infection (UTI) symptoms in the elderly manifests like signs of dementia. Mom was starting to get aggressive towards me, kicking and punching. I figured dementia was worsening; I took her to a neurologist who prescribed Quetiapine which put her in a zombie-like state. I knew that would not work. I then scheduled an appointment with her primary care physician who ordered labs for a UTI. The lab results came back positive and he prescribed antibiotics. After successful treatment she was back to normal. Now, when she starts to get a little snappy or start putting orange peelings into the potted plant, I get her tested for a UTI. So far, I have a 99% success rate.

3. What I learned is that not all incontinent underwear are the same! For some reason mom refused to wear Depends®, she preferred Always Discreet. As time went on she began to urinate straight through them. I was browsing one of those caregiver support group sites and read one woman's post about her frustration with her mother soiling her furniture. Someone responded to her and suggested that she try Abri-Flex incontinent underwear. Well, I gave them a try and they are the best thing ever! However, they are super expensive. I reserve them for when we are going to be away from the home for a few hours, like doctor's appointments or to the hairdresser. The rest of the time I just make sure that the aide takes her to the bathroom about an hour after lunch.

4. My mom got to a point where she wasn't swallowing her medications or food; she just held them in her mouth. I learned from her speech therapist that the term for that behavior is called "pocketing" and is common in dementia patients.

5. I learned that it is a must to have the right supplies on hand: gloves; pre-moistened disposable washcloths; waterproof bed pads (which I also

use to cover her favorite spot on the couch). They can all be ordered on Amazon!

6. I found that caregiver support groups were not beneficial for me. I know the importance of caregiver self-care but, for me, support groups were not the answer. There were very few in my community and I had to block out time to drive the distance and try to find someone to stay with mom while I was gone. They were largely attended by people who had more assistance than I did and I felt they were culturally irrelevant.

7. I learned there are a lot of resources available for low-income and the elderly. One resource that was very helpful was Rebuilding Together DC - Alexandria. They donated and installed a practically new chairlift for us. When it needed repair a couple years later, they sent a repairman. They also installed handrails on the outside deck stairs. There are probably similar organizations in every state.

8. The thing that was most helpful for me was gaining knowledge about assistance for Veteran or Service member family caregivers. I found out that the U.S. Department of Veterans Affairs Program of Comprehensive Assistance for Family Caregivers provides a monthly stipend to Primary Family Caregivers if the veteran or Service member is eligible.

9. Well, I learned that after a while my home would transform from showcase living to waterproof covering on living and dining room furniture; from a fragile figurine to a portable potty; and an antique coffee table replaced by a rollator. But all in all, it has certainly been worth the transformation.

10. More than anything, I learned it is important to have all legal documents in place early. Have an attorney draw up a Durable Power of Attorney versus a General Power of Attorney, because it continues even upon incapacity. A Medical Power of Attorney grants someone the power to make decisions about health care. These documents should be in place before the individual has cognitive decline. It goes without saying that a Will is important, but also include an Advance Directive so that caregivers will know whether the person should be resuscitated in case of serious illness. Seek the advice of an attorney!

Acknowledgements

To my daughter, Dr. La'Tonya Rease Miles whose mere existence has always motivated me to be and do more. Thank you for coming into my life! I also thank you for your keen editorial skills and advice. To my grandchildren, Jabari and Zoe, who inspire me every day to leave a legacy of love, accomplishments, and the confidence to know they have the power to do and become anything.

Thank you to my two Sisters on the Wall who I know always have my back. *Agape!*

Thank you to the 17 contributors to this book for the courage to share your stories and journeys with us; without you there would be no book.

Finally, to my mother: thank you for your sharp wit, generous heart, and the sound wisdom you shared with all who came to seek your counsel. The love in my heart for you is boundless.

To Black family caregivers everywhere, you are always in our hearts and thoughts. The ancestors celebrate your caring Spirit and the Creator acknowledges your unselfish, sacrificial work every second of each day. Stay strong!

To any care recipient mentioned in this book who transitioned to ancestorhood prior to publication, our sincerest condolences to your family and loved ones who celebrated your life and shared your story.

Lastly, one son offered the following statement: "There needs to be some immediate awareness made that it's okay to decide to do your best to take care of your loved one . . . from a male perspective. It doesn't make you weak; it doesn't make you less of a man". For many participants, stigmatization has been associated with Black and racial discrimination or the stigma of women's work. As a survival strategy, the African American population tends to remain unified as a culture or within their ethnic group. This is best exemplified by one participant, who stated: "And I think, you know, the cultural aspect of being Black in America. And being a Black man in America, and the stereotypes around that, you know. How do I . . . like I said, I happen to be very lucky. Um, but I really don't talk to anybody. In our culture, it is a woman that does the work [of caregiving], it's, you know, you're gonna, you're . . . most of friends of mine, their wives take care of their mothers. I think that's got to change; we've got to open up, we've got to evolve in our culture".

Barbara Pollard Deskins, Susan Letvak, Laurie Kennedy-Malone, Pamela Johnson Rowsey, Leandra Bedini and Denise Rhew, the experiences of African American Male Caregivers, 2022

www.ingramcontent.com/pod-product-compliance
Lightning Source LLC
Chambersburg PA
CBHW062045090426
42740CB00016B/3023